SAINTS

A Family Story

John Cavadini *&* Catherine Cavadini
Illustrated by Anastassia Cassady

PARACLETE PRESS
BREWSTER, MASSACHUSETTS

2023 First Printing

Saints: A Family Story

Text copyright © 2023 by John Christopher Cavadini and Catherine Rose Cavadini
Illustrations copyright © 2023 by Anastassia Therese Cassady

ISBN 978-1-64060-754-5

Library of Congress Cataloging-in-Publication Data
Names: Cavadini, John C., author. | Cavadini, Catherine Rose, author. |
    Cassady, Anastassia Therese, 1989- illustrator.
Title: Saints : a family story / by John Christopher Cavadini and Catherine
    Rose Cavadini ; illustrated by Anastassia Therese Cassady.
Description: Brewster, Massachusetts : Paraclete Press, 2023. | Includes
    bibliographical references. | Summary: "The saints are presented as a "Family,"
    living in many different times and places. Some saints learned to love and to live
    the faith through the witness of their own family, other saints formed spiritual families,
    with connections across the centuries"—Provided by publisher.
Identifiers: LCCN 2023000782 (print) | LCCN 2023000783 (ebook) | ISBN
    9781640607545 (hardcover) | ISBN 9781640607552 (epub) | ISBN
    9781640607569 (pdf)
Subjects: LCSH: Christian saints--Biography--Juvenile literature. | BISAC:
    JUVENILE NONFICTION / Religious / Christian / Biography & Autobiography
    (see also Biography & Autobiography / Religious) | JUVENILE NONFICTION /
    Religious / Christian / Values & Virtues
Classification: LCC BX4658 .C38 2023 (print) | LCC BX4658 (ebook) | DDC
    282.092/2--dc23/eng/20230306
LC record available at https://lccn.loc.gov/2023000782
LC ebook record available at https://lccn.loc.gov/2023000783

10 9 8 7 6 5 4 3 2 1

Cover Design: Paraclete Design / Cover Art: Anastassia Therese Cassady

Published by Paraclete Press
Brewster, Massachusetts

www.paracletepress.com

Printed in India

For

My grandchildren, present and future,
and to all grandchildren everywhere.

— JOHN CAVADINI

For

Anna, James, John, and Zelie,
with love from your Mom.

— CATHERINE CAVADINI

For my children,
Genevieve, Ivanka, and Dmitri,
my constant critics, without whom I would have
never received proper illustrative advice.

— ANASTASSIA CASSADY

CONTENTS

Letter to Families   1

Pope Saint John Paul II († 2005)   3

Saint Anna, Prophetess († first century)   5

Saint Joseph († first century)   9

Saint John the Baptist († first century)   11

Saint James the Greater, Apostle († first century)   14

Saint Luke the Evangelist († first century)   19

Saint Ignatius of Antioch († c. 108)   21

Saints Cosmas & Damian († c. 303)   25

Saint Demetrius of Thessalonica († 306)   28

Saint Macrina, the Elder († c. 340)   31

Saint Anthony of Egypt († 356)   35

Saints Monica & Augustine († 387, † 430)   38

Saint Genevieve († 512)   42

Saint Benedict († 547)   47

Blessed Herman of Reichenau († 1054)   50

Saint Bernard of Clairvaux († 1153)   53

Saint Dominic († 1221)   57

Saint Francis of Assisi († 1226)   59

Saint Thomas Aquinas († 1274)   62

Saint Catherine of Siena († 1380)   65

Saint Joan of Arc († 1431)   69

Saint Juan Diego († 1548)   73

Saint Rose of Lima († 1617)   77

Saints Zélie & Louis Martin († 1877, † 1894)   81

Saint Bernadette († 1879)   85

Venerable Augustus Tolton († 1897)   89

Saint Thérèse of Lisieux († 1897)   92

Blessed Pier Giorgio Frassati († 1925)   95

Saint Maximilian Kolbe († 1941)   99

Blessed Franz Jaegerstaetter († 1943)   103

Takashi Nagai, Servant of God († 1951)   106

Saint Gianna Molla († 1962)   109

Dorothy Day, Servant of God († 1980)   112

Saint Teresa of Calcutta († 1997)   115

FOR FURTHER READING   119

Dear Families,

We are so glad to have you join us in telling the stories of the saints! Telling their stories is a beautiful task, especially within our families, who are the domestic Church.

This collection, *Saints: A Family Story*, is composed of stories we have written for our own children (Katie) and grandchildren (John) and friends. They are adapted from Scripture, from original sources within the Tradition, and from the writings of the saints themselves or their family and friends.

The saints are presented as a "Family," living in many different times and places. Just think: many of these saints learned to love and to live the faith through the witness of their parents and grandparents or their brothers and sisters. Other saints form spiritual families, with connections between them found across the centuries.

We begin with the story of Pope Saint John Paul II because he called the Church today to sanctity by giving us the gift of more and more saints. The stories then move chronologically, from stories of saints in the Gospels, to martyrs, confessors, and ascetics of the early Church, to saints of the medieval period, and to more modern saints, including Venerable Augustus Tolton, Blessed Pier Giorgio Frassati, and Saint Teresa of Calcutta.

Through the stories of these saints, we receive new brothers and sisters, mothers and fathers, grandmothers and grandfathers in the faith. Each person's life tells the "story" of God's love in a unique and unrepeatable way. The illustrations bring shape and color to these stories, capturing the true diversity among the magnificent and beautiful "family of saints."

For those wishing to read more, we offer the titles of the books used in writing our stories at the end of the book. Perhaps they will help you to continue sharing the stories of saints as gifts of love with your own families and friends.

Happy reading,
John, Katie, and Tess

Pope Saint John Paul II, "The Great" (1920–2005)

Listen,
Knock, knock, knock!
the even knocking of hammers.
Knock, knock, knock!
Listen!

K AROL JOZEF WOJTYLA worked in a rock quarry, where limestone slabs were cut from the ground with big hammers and electricity. Knock! Knock! Knock!

While he worked, his father was at home, alone. Karol's brother, Edmund, had died, and so had his mother, Emilia. Karol loved his father very much. And when Karol was at home with his father, he felt a different kind of knocking. He watched his father kneel and pray every night. And then he felt the knocking of Christ on his heart.

Karol Jozef Wojtyla was Saint John Paul II's name before he became Pope. His parents, Karol and Emilia, had named him Karol Jozef when he was born on May 18, 1920, in Wadowice, Poland. When Pope John Paul II was still the little boy called Karol, he loved to play sports with his friends and to write poetry. He wanted to grow up and become an actor.

But he had to do his acting in secret because plays and theater were not allowed. After the Nazis invaded Poland in 1939, the Polish people were not free to live as they wished, but only as the Nazis allowed them to live. They required Karol to work in the rock quarry instead of the theater. But he wasn't afraid! He and his friends performed their favorite plays in secret in their living rooms.

In fact, they had to do almost everything in secret. Even going to Mass had to be a secret. In 1942 Karol went to the seminary in secret. Studying to be a priest was not

allowed by the Nazis either. But, remember, Karol wasn't afraid! He became a priest anyway, and was ordained on All Saints Day in 1946.

Thirty-two years later, in October 1978, Karol became Pope John Paul II. His first message to the Church that night was not to be afraid anymore! Be free, he said. And love! "Open wide the doors to Christ, and be not afraid of him!" Knock! Knock! Knock! As Pope, John Paul II taught us that every human being is loved by God and is always totally free. This should not be a "secret"! No, he must tell the whole world! Knock! Knock! Knock!

One of the ways he decided to tell the whole world was to name new saints. The saints, for John Paul II, were people who were not afraid to love God or to love others as freely and as completely as God loved them. During his time as Pope, John Paul II canonized 482 new saints and beatified over 1300 new blesseds! These saints offer examples of brave and heroic love from all walks of life: teachers and students, lawyers, farmers, seamstresses, doormen, composers and musicians, policemen, artists, doctors and nurses, journalists, scientists, soldiers, slaves—all sorts of religious and lay people. And they included such well-known names as Maximilian Kolbe, Gianna Molla, Josephine Bakhita, Juan Diego, Andrew Kim, and Mother Teresa.

Sometimes John Paul II would spend entire days in conversation with God and His friends, the saints, especially Jesus's Mother, Mary. Not only would he kneel as his father had, but he would even lie on the stone floor of the church, arms spread out like the Cross.

Today John Paul II is himself recognized by the Church as a saint. He was canonized in 2014 by Pope Francis, just nine years after his death in 2005. Pope Emeritus Benedict XVI suggested we call Pope Saint John Paul II "The Great," for his heroic work sharing the Good News of God's love for us.

Saint Anna, Prophetess
(† first century)

SAINT ANNA is one of the most beautiful saints in the whole Bible. We read about her in the Gospel of Luke. Anna got married when she was young and lived with her husband for seven years. They were very happy, but then, very sadly, he died. We don't know how. So Anna was a widow at a young age. She observed the days of fasting very carefully, perhaps because fasting is a sign of mourning.

FEAST DAY

February

3

Anna never married again. Maybe she missed her husband too much. She doesn't seem to have had any children. She had loved the Temple since she was a child, and she began to visit the Temple to pray there by herself. Little by little she spent more and more time in the Temple because she really loved being in God's house. There she shared her sadness with the Lord in her prayers.

After a while Anna stayed longer and longer in the Temple until she finally stayed there all the time. In the Gospel of Luke we are told that "she never left the Temple, but worshiped there with fasting and prayer night and day" (Lk. 2:37). This is a very beautiful memory we have of Anna. God listened to her and showed her the beauty of His love. She became a friend of God, who comforted Anna over the loss of her husband and began secretly to show her many things of greater and greater beauty while she was praying. That is how she became a prophetess. God trusted her to speak for Him!

One of the beautiful things God showed to Anna was how a new King would come to comfort her, and the people of Israel, and all the world. When Anna was 84 years old, Mary and Joseph brought the baby Jesus to the Temple to be blessed. Anna was there, where she always was, waiting to welcome Him. Seeing the baby Jesus filled her with joy! She greeted Mary, Joseph, and Jesus, and at that very hour she gave thanks to God, and "began to speak about the child, Jesus" (Lk. 2:38).

Anna, who had seen many things of great beauty from God, recognized Jesus as the King that God had promised to send to comfort and save all the Holy People. She had spent her life praying and waiting for Him to come. She was rewarded with this joy of seeing Jesus, of thanking God for Him and of prophesying to everyone she met about their King. And now, we can join Anna in her joy: "Break forth together into singing, for the Lord has comforted his people … and all the ends of the earth shall see the salvation of our God" (Isa. 52.9-10).

ITE AD JOSEPH

Saint Joseph
(† first century)

SAINT JOSEPH is the husband of Mary. Jesus is the Son of God, our Father in Heaven, and has no earthly father, but since Saint Joseph is the husband of Mary, he is the one on earth that God chose for His own Son to call "Dad!"

An angel revealed to Saint Joseph that God had chosen him for this important job, but Saint Joseph never bragged about it to anyone. In fact, he never talked about how important he was. He never says even one word in the Bible. He didn't care too much about talking, because he loved to listen instead. He loved to listen to God, who speaks in the Scriptures and in His Law. He was such a good listener he could recognize God's voice even in a dream. He loved to listen to Mary, whom he knew God loved so much that He chose her to be the mother of Jesus. And Saint Joseph was so pleased and delighted to listen to Jesus chatter as a little guy, the very One whom God had chosen Saint Joseph to watch over.

The Bible says that Joseph was a "just man" (Matt. 1:19). Being a just man means Joseph was always attentive to the Lord and was faithful to whatever the Lord asked of him. Saint Joseph loved listening so much that he heard the voice of the angel in a dream that warned him to take the little baby Jesus and His Mother to Egypt, to escape King Herod, who wished to do them harm. He could hear God's voice even in a dream because he loved Him so much and was hoping to do whatever the Lord asked of him as soon as he knew what it was. Right away Joseph took his little family out of Bethlehem and onto the long, long road to Egypt. They had to walk this long road because they were poor! But Saint Joseph didn't mind, because it was something God asked him to do and he loved doing the will of the Lord. It made him happy—too happy even to talk, at least a lot of the time.

There are legends that say the Egyptians loved this little family. Joseph was a carpenter, and maybe he could earn a living while they were there. But soon enough it was

safe to travel back home, and again in a dream, God told Joseph it was safe. So he took his family home.

We know Saint Joseph taught Jesus to love God, just as he, Saint Joseph, did. The Bible doesn't tell us anything about Jesus's life at home with Mary and Joseph, but it does invite us to use our imaginations to think of it. We imagine that Saint Joseph taught Jesus how to be a carpenter. We can also imagine how the Holy Family was at home, working together: Jesus helps Saint Joseph saw boards; Mary spins wool. Saint Joseph, who is of the royal house of David the King, is wearing his royal, purple robe. In some images of Saint Joseph, he is hiding his purple robe. He doesn't brag about how important he is! But at home, Jesus and Mary know how important he is to them. He can be himself without explaining. He can wear his purple robe, reminding Jesus that He too is of the House of David, and that He will be the King of the Universe!

We do not know how Saint Joseph died, but when Jesus was grown up and preaching and teaching, only His mother was mentioned. We imagine that Saint Joseph had died before then. He died with Jesus and Mary with him—the perfectly happy death! So we call Saint Joseph the patron saint of a happy death.

We also call Saint Joseph the Protector of the Universal Church, of the *whole* Church, because he cared for and fed the one who was to be Head of the Church, Jesus. The bread that Saint Joseph earned fed Jesus, the Bread of Life!

So in a way, Saint Joseph is our Dad too, because he is the earthly Dad of Jesus Christ, in whose life we share. Once, for example, a sister found Saint Bernadette crying. She asked her why. It was because her own father, whom she loved very much, had died back home and no one had even told her! She said, though, that she was comforted because now she would have Saint Joseph as her father, and she visited Saint Joseph's chapel every day and prayed to him. He is our spiritual father, too!

Saint John the Baptist
(† first century)

SAINT JOHN did not live in a house. He did not live in a town or a village. He lived in the wilderness. No food grows in the wild desert—not even one plant grows there. But John didn't care. He wasn't looking for food in the desert. He read in the Bible that God likes the desert and so he thought he could find God there. He lived near the Jordan River because he knew in the Bible it was called the River of God. He found locusts and wild honey near the River, and he knew that God was taking care of him.

John wanted his heart to be empty of everything, like the desert, so God would like it there too. God filled his heart with a vision. He saw a dove coming down from the sky and touching the head of a young man who also came to the River of God. A voice from Heaven said that the man on whom the dove would land was God's beloved Son. John knew from this that God wanted him to stay by the river and watch for this man.

Other people discovered him at the Jordan and asked him how they could find God too. He told them to make their hearts a place for God by being sorry for their sins, and he told them that a sign for their sorrow would be if they went with him into the River Jordan and the water would wash away their sins. (This is why we call him "John the Baptist.") All of a sudden among the people who came to be baptized was a young man like the one he saw in his vision. John knew this was the Son of God. He saw the dove come down on His head and heard the voice of the Father from the sky saying, "This is my Beloved Son." It was Jesus!

John told Jesus that He did not need to be baptized. Jesus told him to baptize Him anyway, because He wanted to keep everyone company who was in the River and who were sad because of their sins. He wanted them to know that God loved them and that He would never abandon them. So John baptized Jesus too. Jesus went up out of the River and began to heal people and comfort them.

Later on, John was arrested. The King, King Herod, did not like John because John had scolded him for his sins. But Herod would not be baptized. Instead he put John in a dark prison. King Herod's wife told him he should kill John for criticizing him. She told her daughter to ask Herod to bring John the Baptist's head to her on a plate. Herod ordered his soldiers to behead John in the prison and to bring his head back on a platter.

When Jesus heard that his friend John was killed, he said that there was no greater holy person that had lived up to that time in the whole world. Jesus said that John the Baptist had been predicted by the prophet Isaiah, who wrote that there will come a voice crying out in the wilderness to prepare the Way of the Lord (Isa. 40:3). Jesus said that is what John did. John prepared Christ's way and cried out to everyone to believe in Him.

Did you know that John and Jesus were also cousins? John was the baby who leapt in Elizabeth's womb at the Annunciation. He had known the joy of the Incarnation and had begun to prepare Christ's way even before he was born.

John the Baptist prays for all of us, so we can prepare the way of the Lord in our own hearts. We do this every time we say a prayer, even a very short one!

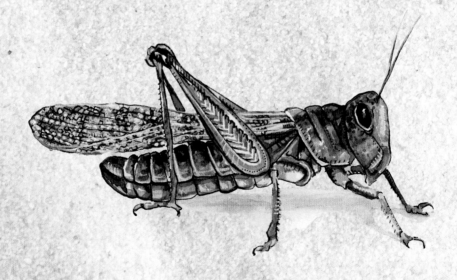

Saint James the Greater, Apostle
(† first century)

SAINT JAMES was one of the Twelve Apostles. He was chosen to be an Apostle by Jesus! James became one of Jesus's most trusted friends, along with James's brother John and their friend Peter.

But James didn't start out to be an Apostle. He and his brother John worked for their dad, whose name was Zebedee. They were fishermen. They had special boats with a special kind of net and they went out on the Sea of Galilee to let their nets down and catch whatever fish they could.

Zebedee and his sons were partners in a business with a neighboring family, who also had two sons who were fishermen, Peter and Andrew. Their father was named John (John 1:42).

Here is what the Gospel of Matthew says:

As Jesus walked by the Sea of Galilee, he saw two brothers, Simon who is called Peter and Andrew his brother, casting a net into the sea—for they were fishermen. And he said to them, "Follow me, and I will make you fish for people." Immediately they left their nets and followed him. As he went from there, he saw two other brothers, James the son of Zebedee and John his brother, in the boat with their father Zebedee, mending their nets, and he called them. Immediately they left the boat and their father, and followed him.
—Matthew 4:18–22

Jesus knew that James would follow Him if He asked him, along with the other brothers. He knew that that was all He had to do—to ask him. The Gospel of Luke says that Jesus worked a miracle, helping Peter and Andrew catch an amazing number of fish for their dad, and James and John saw the miracle happen. That was when they all decided to follow Jesus, even leaving their dad in the boat, to run the business himself, perhaps with John, father of Peter and Andrew. But Jesus knew that James would follow Him, with or without a miracle.

These two pairs of brothers and friends followed Jesus everywhere and learned everything about Him. James and John loved Jesus so much that they asked Him if they could sit right next to Him, eventually, in Heaven. Peter, James, and John were with Jesus in the Garden of Gethsemane, when it was night, and Jesus knew that His enemies were going to sneak up and arrest Him. Peter, James, and John also were brought by Jesus on a trail leading up to the top of a high mountain, and they saw Jesus transfigured, shining with light and talking to two ancient saints, Moses and Elijah. How lucky they were!

But people love Saint James because he was brave. He and his brother John were nicknamed "sons of thunder" (Mk. 3:17). They followed Jesus closely and later fearlessly proclaimed His resurrection to everyone. After Jesus's death and Resurrection, James went to Spain to preach the Gospel there. That was a long trip from Israel. After spending so much time in a boat, James now had to journey all the way to Spain. And instead of catching fish, James became a "fisher of men," joyfully telling them the good news of Jesus.

When James returned to Jerusalem he was killed by King Herod, who persecuted the Church, hoping to destroy it. But his body was carried back to Spain, where it was buried. Now, in honor of the long walk of Saint James to preach in Spain, many pilgrims walk part of the same road, praying the whole way! They walk to his tomb, in Compostela.

Saint Luke the Evangelist
(† first century)

 AINT LUKE loved to tell stories. He also loved adventures. We know this because he wrote many stories about his adventures with Saint Paul. Luke was also a doctor. He traveled with Saint Paul and his friends as they preached the gospel in many different cities and towns. He cared for them if they were ever injured.

FEAST DAY

October
18

In each town, Saint Paul told everyone about the Lord Jesus, how He loved them and had suffered for them and been raised from the dead. Many people believed and wanted to be baptized. But others were not as friendly. Luke tells us stories about how he and Paul and friends were arrested and put in jail. One time, they were locked up in jail for the night. They began to sing hymns to praise God anyway! Suddenly, Luke tells us, there was a great earthquake that shook the whole prison. The doors were broken open!

In another adventure, Paul and Luke were sailing to Rome. Dark clouds came up and a terrible storm began to toss their ship with wind and waves. The ship began to split apart! Luckily, there was land nearby, the island of Malta. Saint Paul, Saint Luke, and everyone else swam through the stormy sea to safety. Whew!

Luke listened carefully to all the stories that Paul and his friends told about Jesus. He loved to hear the stories. He began to have an idea. "What if I could write my own story about Jesus? Then everyone could read about Him and love Him as much as I do!" He began to seek out old friends and relatives of Jesus. He asked them to tell him their stories. He took notes. When he was ready, he wrote everything down from start to finish. We still have the story he wrote. We call it "The Gospel according to Saint Luke." You can find it in the Bible.

Luke did his work very carefully. He tells us stories that none of the other Gospels tell us. For example, he tells us about the two men traveling to the village called Emmaus after Jesus was crucified. They were sad because Jesus had been killed. They did not know He had been raised from the dead. Luke tells us how Jesus appeared to them in disguise and

walked with them and began to console them. When they stopped to eat, Luke tells us that Jesus took bread and blessed it and broke it and they immediately recognized Him! They were overjoyed!

Luke also tells us stories that Jesus told. Many are not in the other Gospels. For example, he tells Jesus's story of the poor man Lazarus and the rich man who had no pity on him. When they died, Father Abraham received the poor man into Heaven and comforted him. Luke also tells us the story of the Good Samaritan, who was traveling and on the road found a man who had been beaten up. Instead of walking by, he had pity on him. He picked him up and took him to an inn. He paid the innkeeper to care for him. Perhaps because he was a doctor, Luke liked best to remember Jesus's stories about people who took care of their neighbors in trouble.

Most of all, Luke tells us stories about the Blessed Mother that no other evangelist records. Only Luke tells us, in his loving way, about the angel Gabriel who came to Mary. Only Luke tells us about Mary's visit to Elizabeth. Only Luke tells us about Mary and Joseph's trip to Bethlehem, and how Jesus was born there and placed in a manger. Only Luke tells us about the angels who announced His birth with great joy to the shepherds.

How did Luke know these stories? The Blessed Mother is the only one who could have known about the angel Gabriel's visit. Luke tells us that Mary pondered all that happened in her heart. She kept these stories alive. Perhaps she told everything that was in her heart to Saint Luke! The stories are so full of beauty and love that they seem like paintings that help us to see everything as Mary saw them. One way that Luke is remembered is as a painter of beautiful pictures, even if what he painted with was words and not actual paint.

Saint Luke invites everyone to love adventures the way he did. He wants everyone to have the adventure of loving Jesus in their own lives. He hopes we will then tell our own stories, just like he did!

Saint Ignatius *of* Antioch
(† c. 108)

FEAST DAY
———
October
17

To Mary, the Christ-Bearer

Strengthen and console me, a disciple of your John, from whom I have learned many things about your Jesus, things wondrous to tell, and I am greatly astonished at hearing them. Assure me of these amazing things, for you were always so intimately close to Jesus and shared his secrets. This is my heart's desire.

Farewell, and let us be strengthened in the faith, with you, through you, and in you.

From Your Ignatius

To my beloved fellow disciple, Ignatius:

The things you have heard and learned from John are true. Believe them, hold on to them, be steadfast in being a Christian; shape your whole life on what you have learned. I will come to visit you with John. Stand firm and be strong in the faith. Do not let hardships shake you, and may your spirit be strong and joyful in God. Amen!

The humble handmaid of Jesus Christ

E KNOW ABOUT SAINT IGNATIUS OF ANTIOCH from the letters he wrote. In fact, we don't know anything about his life before he started writing letters! Saint Bernard of Clairvaux tells us about his letters to Jesus's Mother, Mary. Mary wrote back to Saint Ignatius with all the tenderness of a mother. Ignatius wrote the letter above to Our Lady earlier in his life, when he was learning about Jesus from Saint John, the Beloved Disciple and Evangelist in the ancient land of Syria. Maybe you remember that after Jesus died, John took Mary into his own home, and they took care of each other as mother and son. This is how Ignatius met Mary through his teacher, John. Mary became a mother in faith to Ignatius, too! Wouldn't it be nice to get a letter in the mail from Mary? And then for her to visit your house with John the Evangelist?

Ignatius followed the advice Mary gave him in her letter. We learn from his later letters that he was strong in his faith, strong enough even for martyrdom. He believed God showed his love for us in Jesus, and so he tried to imitate Jesus in everything he said and did, even His death, so as to teach God's love to others.

Ignatius became the bishop of Antioch in Syria. Bishops have the important job of teaching others about Jesus and the Christian faith. Ignatius did this in the letters he wrote. He often wrote about Christmas, when God truly became a human being to be with us and to love us. Ignatius knew it was hard to believe God loved us this much, and he wanted to encourage everyone just as Mary had encouraged him. And so Ignatius told everyone again and again the wonderful things about Jesus, just as he had learned them from John.

But sometimes Ignatius ran out of words. Once he wrote that he had no words to describe the brilliance of the Christmas star. It was too beautiful!

Ignatius also told everyone that they don't always need words. Ignatius liked silence. He was like Saint Joseph in this way. He liked teaching people about God's love by loving them. Ignatius encouraged the faithful to do good things for one another as quickly and as often as they could.

Because they were written so long ago, we do not have all the letters Ignatius wrote. We do have the ones he sent to the churches along his journey from Antioch to Rome, where he would be martyred. These were the last seven letters he wrote, and he had to write them with handcuffs on. But Ignatius was joyful anyway! He said his chains were like "precious pearls" because they reminded him of Jesus's love, shown in Jesus's own arrest in the Garden of Gethsemane.

As a martyr Ignatius also imitated Christ in his death. This is what a martyr does! Ignatius had to be very brave because the Emperor made him fight with lions, and that is how Ignatius died. But love is stronger than death (Song of Songs 8:6).

Saint John the Evangelist tells us that when Christ had died on the Cross, a soldier pierced His side, revealing His heart. Even in this Ignatius was like Christ: they say that after Ignatius's death, they could see the name of Jesus written on his heart in gold letters! We can see it too, in the way Ignatius loved Jesus with all his heart!

Saints Cosmas & Damian
(† c. 303)

OSMAS AND DAMIAN were twin brothers, born sometime around AD 250. They were the oldest of five brothers. The three younger brothers were named Anthimus, Leontius, and Euprepius. Their wealthy parents died young, and the five boys inherited their money.

All the boys had been brought up as Christians by their parents. They had learned from them to love the Lord Jesus. When their parents died, the boys, especially the two eldest, wondered what they should do with their lives. When they went outside their own beautiful home, they saw the misery of people who had no money, and no faith to comfort them. Cosmas and Damian decided they would study medicine together. They thought that if they were able to heal people's bodies, they could also comfort their souls, teaching them through the Christian faith that God loved them.

They also decided that since their parents had left them enough money, they could be doctors for everyone, including the poor and the miserable, without charging any fees. They believed their parents, whom they loved, would have wanted them to act this way. They remembered their parents' generosity to them, and they knew the words of our Lord: "Heal the sick, raise the dead, cleanse those who have leprosy, drive out demons. You received without payment; give without payment" (Matt. 10:8). So they began their careers, always working together as brothers. The little brothers looked up to their two big brothers, and decided they would help their older brothers in their practice.

We know that around the year 300, the Emperor, whose name was Diocletian, decided to try to stamp out all the Christians living in the Roman Empire. The brothers were working as doctors in the Eastern part of the Empire in an area called "Syria." The Roman Governor of Syria, whose name was Lysias, heard about Cosmas and Damian. He heard about them because, since they never took any money from anyone, they were very popular. People loved them, especially the poor and the sick left to die out in the street.

All of these people wanted to know why the two doctors were so generous. Cosmas and Damian explained to them about the Lord Jesus, who was the Son of God, and how He loved the poor and healed them. Jesus never took any payment. Instead, He gave up the most precious thing of all, more precious than money, His own body and blood, out of love for all people, to save them from loneliness and death. They told them about how, even though He was killed, He had risen from the dead on the third day, and how He would welcome all the dead into Heaven with Him, especially those who tried to love people in the same way He did.

Many of the poor people they healed had never heard that anybody loved them. They certainly never heard that there was a God who cared about them even when everyone else treated them so terribly. They wanted to become Christians themselves. So many of them did do that, that the Governor heard about it and was furious! Lysias, the Governor, decided to arrest Cosmas and Damian. He told them to stop being Christians or they would be killed. They refused. They loved the Lord Jesus too much to say they hated Him or to forget about Him. They were very brave! The little brothers all rushed to help their older brothers. So they were arrested too! After a short trial, all of them were beheaded and they died together.

We know that many, many people loved them and began to pray to them after their death. We know this because their names are included in a very ancient prayer that we still say at Mass on many Sundays, the First Eucharistic Prayer, the oldest one of the four Eucharistic Prayers.

Many stories were told about these saints, and all of them show how much they were loved. They all tell us something about their generous spirit and their love for each other since they always worked together as brothers. One story tells about how they healed a wealthy sick woman. She was so grateful she wanted to reward them. But they refused to take any money, because, they said, they worked for their King, the Lord Jesus. She asked them at least to take something small as a gift, and she offered them a bag with three eggs in it. They refused, but before they left the woman took Damian aside and pleaded with him, in the Name of the Lord Jesus, to accept this small token of gratitude to the Lord. So he did.

But when Cosmas found out, he was angry with his brother! He would not even sleep in the same room with his brothers. He said that his twin brother, Damian, had broken their rule to not accept payment for their work. But guess what! In the night, the Lord Jesus appeared to Cosmas in a dream! He was smiling kindly, but He asked why Cosmas was so angry. Cosmas said that his brother had broken the rule they had agreed on. The Lord said, "But he did it because the woman asked him to take it for Me, in My Name, and that is why he took it. I am so pleased with both of you for honoring My Holy Name." Then Cosmas woke up. He ran to his brother's bed and told him what had happened and asked his forgiveness. Of course, Damian was glad, and forgave him! They both then understood that they were partners not only in their own name as brothers, but in the Name of Jesus the Lord and in their love for Him and His love for them.

The two brothers are the patron saints of doctors and nurses and anyone who works in health care. Many people who pray to these saintly martyrs have reported miracles occurring in response. The twins Cosmas and Damian are now loved all over the world!

Saint Demetrius
of Thessalonica
(270–306)

SAINT DEMETRIUS is also known as the Myrrh-Gusher. What an interesting name! Maybe you know what myrrh is from the story of the Three Kings who come at Epiphany. One of them brings the baby Jesus a gift of myrrh—an aromatic used to make fragrant incense and oils, like those used at Baptism, Confirmation, and Ordination. Maybe, then, you also already know what myrrh smells like. Have you ever smelled a baby after a Baptism? If so, you have smelled myrrh, and it smells like Heaven! But why is Saint Demetrius called the Myrrh-Gusher? Because his relics have been "gushing" myrrh for more than 1,400 years!

Saint Demetrius was born in Thessalonica in 270. It was against the law to be a Christian at that time, and so his parents kept their Christianity a secret. They baptized Demetrius in a church hidden in their home, marking him then with the scent of myrrh. Demetrius's father was the proconsul, or governor, of Thessalonica, and could provide Demetrius with an excellent education. When his father died, the Emperor made Demetrius the new governor. The Emperor charged Demetrius with the particular task of stamping out Christianity, not knowing Demetrius was himself a Christian.

As proconsul Demetrius no longer kept his Christian faith a secret. He wanted the Law of Love to rule his people, and so he publicly preached the Gospel, bringing many of his citizens to Christ, marking them with myrrh-scented oils during their baptisms.

The Emperor was not happy! On his way home from one of his wars the Emperor decided to stop in Thessalonica and see for himself what was happening. He had Demetrius arrested, and he locked him up in the basement of the Bath House (the building where people would gather to soak in pools of cold or warm water). He then set up many festive games in Thessalonica's stadium for everyone's entertainment. In particular, the Emperor challenged the people to fight with a giant-sized man named Lyaeus, on a

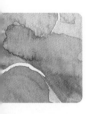

platform suspended over spikes and spears. One day a young Christian, Nestor, decided to fight Lyaeus, and so he went to Demetrius for a blessing. In the basement of the Baths, Demetrius signed Nestor with the Cross. Nestor, in a battle reminiscent of David and Goliath, was victorious!

But Nestor was martyred as soon as the Emperor learned that Demetrius had helped him. And then the Emperor sent soldiers to the Baths to martyr Demetrius, too. Thus, before Demetrius became known as the Myrrh-Gusher, he was called "The Great Martyr Demetrius." He who had brought so many Thessalonians to the Faith, was now marked by both the chrismatic myrrh of Baptism and the "baptism of blood."

After his death, the Christians of Thessalonica began to pray to Demetrius, asking him to protect them and their city when they had to go into battle just as Nestor had asked Demetrius to bless him before his fight. As the years unfolded Saint Demetrius saved Thessalonica from many invasions, battles, and diseases. This is why icons of Saint Demetrius often depict him dressed as a warrior, riding on a horse, and with a spear raised in his hand (much like the images of the well-known Saint George). While Demetrius was a governor and not a warrior, the images of the armor-clad Demetrius are still true images of Demetrius's great works. Saint Paul had once written to the Thessalonians to encourage them to put on "the breastplate of faith and love, and for a helmet the hope of salvation" (1 Thess. 5:8). Saint Demetrius had worn such "armor" in defense of the Gospel against the Emperor. He desired to see everyone baptized and marked with a myrrh-scented cross so that the love of God might become "a spring of water gushing up to eternal life" (John 4:14) in every Christian clad in faith, hope, and love.

Saint Macrina, the Elder
(c. 270–c. 340)

FEAST DAY

January
14

E KNOW SAINT MACRINA through the memories of her grandchildren. They tell us that during the persecution of Christians under the Emperor Diocletian, Saint Macrina the Elder and her husband (whose name we do not know) fled from their home in Pontus, leaving everything behind. They escaped to the mountains near the Black Sea where the forests are so thick and deep that there are many excellent hiding places. Saint Macrina and her husband lived in these thickets for seven years! They had no warm bed and only the fir, birch, and chestnut trees to be their house. Saint Macrina's grandchildren also tell us that God provided for them in the wilderness. He even made sure they had good things to eat! In this way, Saint Macrina came to love God all the more in the thickets by the Black Sea.

Macrina's grandchildren loved her very much. They loved to tell this story about her life in the wilderness, though they didn't really need to: their grandmother was already famous as a "confessor" for her extraordinary witness of faith. More importantly, they told her story with their lives, each imitating her in their own way. Saint Macrina's grandchildren carried her "confession" wherever they went, bearing it as a gift for everyone they met.

Three of Macrina's grandchildren became saints: Saint Basil the Great (of Caesarea), Saint Gregory of Nyssa, and Saint Macrina, who was named after her grandmother. Sts. Basil and Gregory were bishops, as was their youngest brother, Peter of Sebaste. The younger Saint Macrina, their sister, stayed at home her whole life, where she lived with her mother, Emilia—also a saint! Together they made their home into a place of prayer and hospitality—a sort of monastery, or even a sort of "thicket," in which men and women could find shelter and seek God. We also know about their brother Naucratius. He didn't become a priest like his brothers; rather, he went into the wilderness like his grandmother! Naucratius lived as a hermit by the Iris River and cared for the elderly by bringing them fresh-caught fish.

In all of these ways the children and grandchildren lived and magnified the confession of their grandmother. Saint Macrina's love for God was given by Basil to the faithful of Caesarea, by Gregory to the faithful in Nyssa, and by Peter to the faithful of Sebaste; Macrina and Emilia gave it to those who came to their Monastery, and Naucratius gave it to the elderly with whom he also shared his fish. Saint Macrina's "thicket" by the Black Sea was now growing all over the world! Of course, it wasn't growing as fir and birch and chestnut trees. It was growing in all the people who had been told her story as it was confessed in the lives and the love of her grandchildren.

Saint Anthony *of* Egypt
(251–356)

AINT ANTHONY was born in January 251. He was born in Egypt, near the River Nile, and he spent his whole life in Egypt. We do not know his parents' names, but we know that they died when he was about 20 years old. They were farmers, and Anthony inherited the farm.

FEAST DAY

January
17

But Anthony wanted to do something different in life. He wasn't sure what it was.

One day in church he heard the Gospel read, and he heard this verse: "If you wish to be perfect, go, sell your possessions, and give the money to the poor, and you will have treasure in heaven; then come, follow me" (Matt. 19:21).

Anthony thought, "That's me! I want to be perfect, just like the Lord says!" So he sold the farm, and gave away all of the money to the poor, though he saved some for his sister, who went to live with some nuns.

"Now what?" he wondered. He decided he wanted to be a fighter. He wanted to learn to fight against evil and against the devil. How could he learn that? He decided to live with some hermits who were dwelling in the neighborhood, each by themselves. They came together for work and for prayer. Anthony learned from them how to be a fighter.

He trained himself to be very tough. He ate only bread and water, and vegetables sometimes. He fought even harder against the desire to hate anybody or to be angry. He learned to desire God so greatly that he stayed awake praying into the night and got up early to pray some more. Little by little, he learned how to fight against evil, how to be patient, how to not judge people he didn't like, how to not care about being rich or even about having any money at all. He slept on a hard mat.

After 15 years of training, he decided he was tough enough to fight the devil, if the devil wanted to fight. He went out into the desert, where there was a large tomb, like a little stone house. He locked himself in and asked one of his old friends to bring him bread and water once a day. Then he started to pray. Sure enough, the devil, who does not like prayer, came to try to scare him and to fight him, so that he would give up and go home. Anthony told everyone that the devil appeared in the form of many wild animals, like lions, tigers, wolves, snakes, and leopards. They made a terrible lot of noise and threatened to tear him apart. Anthony just kept praying. Eventually the devil got discouraged and left, and the frightening visions stopped. Anthony saw a beam of light from heaven shine into the tomb, and he heard a voice from heaven telling him he had fought well.

Another time the devil came with whips and scourges to beat him and whip him. He did beat Anthony up, but Anthony was very tough by now and sat and prayed through the whole thing. The devil finally stopped and left. The devil was embarrassed to be defeated by someone who had flesh and blood and was not a spirit.

But the devil did not give up. One day Anthony was walking outside his tomb when he saw some gold coins lying on the road. He knew immediately they were not real, because no one ever walked on that road but him. He made the sign of the cross over them, and they disappeared. That is because Anthony was so strong now, that he didn't care about money at all, and so you could not fool him with fake money. Another time the devil came in the shape of a very tall man. Anthony by now could recognize him no matter what form he took, and he made the sign of the cross, and told him to "Beat it!" The devil disappeared in a puff of smoke. Anthony told all of his friends not to be afraid of the devil, and to make the sign of the cross. The devil hates Jesus's cross and fears it, he said, and he will go away immediately.

Anthony decided, after fighting the devil for about 20 years of fighting like this, to go farther into the desert, and he picked a mountain near the Red Sea. He knew he was tough enough to live there. He lived there alone for 45 years. The devil knew better than to mess with him, and stopped coming.

But many people did travel through the desert to see Anthony. Everyone knew that he was almost "perfect." He fought against evil by training himself to love everyone, even people he didn't like. The devil hates love, because that is what makes people strong against him. Everyone knew that Anthony was a very patient and loving man, and they wanted his help.

Anthony received anyone who traveled out to see him. He gave them good advice. He consoled them if they were in grief. He strengthened them if they were suffering from temptations to sin. He was like a doctor for the soul, and he did not charge anything.

Sometimes miracles occurred as a result of his prayers for people. He was like everyone's dad, and people called him "Father!"

Anthony predicted the day of his death. He told his friends who had come to see him to bury him in the desert, secretly, where no one would know where his grave was. He wanted to fight until the end. His final fight was the fight to keep his grave from becoming a place of pilgrimage, which would have made him famous. He fought to stay humble. He died in January 356. That's right, he lived more than 100 years! His fighting had made his body tough too! What "treasures" do you think he found in Heaven?

Saints Monica & Augustine
(331–387) | (354–430)

FEAST DAYS

August
27
&
August
28

UGUSTINE was restless. He kept looking and looking, and always in the wrong places. Augustine's mother, Monica, was restless, too. But she was restless because she wanted to help her son find what he was looking for.

What was Augustine looking for? He was looking for love. Augustine was searching for a love that is given so completely that you know it is yours forever. Then he could stop looking and rest. Then he would be happy.

Monica knew that the kind of love Augustine was searching for was God's love. And so she knew where to find it: in the Church. In the Church God gives Himself to us in the Eucharist. Monica prayed and prayed that her son would stop looking for God's love everywhere else — in books, in games, in good grades, in his friends — and look in the Church instead.

But Augustine spent many years looking everywhere else. Later in life, Augustine remembered all his futile looking, and he wrote about it in a book called *The Confessions*. There, Augustine tells us about all the ways he was mistaken about where to look for love and happiness. He remembered one time when he was out with his friends at night. They saw a magnificent pear tree in their neighbor's yard, heavy with pears. They decided to sneak into their neighbor's yard and pick the pears. But they didn't eat them; they just took them and threw them away! Augustine thought he would be happy doing the things his friends thought were fun. But he wasn't happy; he was sad and restless! So many things in Augustine's life made him feel this way, even when he had grown up and had become the most prestigious professor in Milan . . . and in the whole Empire!

Augustine also remembered how much his mother prayed for him. He looked at his mother and suddenly saw a woman of great faith and humility. He saw how his mother loved the Church and how she received the Eucharist every single day. He saw that this made her happy and that it helped her make other people happy, too. She truly loved God! Augustine became so grateful for the gift of his mother's example! He realized that when he looked at her, he looked at the Church!

One day, Augustine was talking with his mother about what life must be like for the saints in Heaven. Their conversation was like a prayer. They forgot their worries and their restlessness, and they experienced together the great gift of God's love. They were at rest and happy, filled with a beautiful vision of God's love and all His saints in Heaven.

Monica died soon after this experience. Augustine was very sad! But he was also very glad that his mother was at rest with God and all the saints. He continued to follow his mother's example all his life, happy to receive Christ in the Eucharist. He prayed for her whenever he approached the altar.

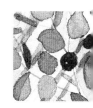

Augustine became the bishop of a city in Northern Africa called Hippo. He spent much of his time in Hippo teaching the faithful about the Church and the sacraments. He also still liked to study books, but now he studied the books of Scripture. He especially liked the beautiful stories about creation in the Book of Genesis. When he died in August of 430, he was reading the Psalms, which he had asked a friend to put on the walls of his bedroom. Thus, he spent his last days praying in bed. "Find rest, O my soul, in God alone" (see Psalm 62:5).

Saint Genevieve
(c. 419–c. 512)

A VERY IMPORTANT VISITOR WAS COMING TO NANTERRE. Seven-year-old Genevieve, her golden hair in braids, ran through the streets as fast as her little legs could carry her. She wanted to see the bishop of Auxerre!

But so did everyone else. The streets were full of people, all crowding together to welcome Bishop Germain and to hear him preach.

Genevieve listened attentively. In fact, she listened so well that Bishop Germain noticed this little girl amongst the whole crowd. After his sermon, he found Genevieve and asked her if she would like to give her life to God. Genevieve was radiant. "Yes! I would!" came her happy reply.

Before Bishop Germain left Nanterre the next day, he gave Genevieve a necklace with a simple medal on it that was engraved with a cross. From then on, she wore this medal every day as a reminder of how she had given her life to God.

When Genevieve was 15 her parents, Severus and Geroncia, died, and so she went to Paris to live with her godmother, Lutetia.

Genevieve often spoke with the angels and the saints. Talking with the angels and saints was quite natural for someone who prayed so much, but other people did not understand. Some people were even jealous, and so they were very mean to Genevieve.

But Genevieve continued in her happy ways and in her works of charity. She knew people were unkind to Jesus and that He continued to do good and marvelous things for them. Genevieve would do marvelous things, too!

Once, the city of Paris was surrounded by the Frankish army. The Parisians were cut off from their usual supplies of food. They were starving! Genevieve decided she must do something, and so, praying for Christ's protection, she set sail on the Seine River, leading a whole fleet of ships to the city of Troyes. At Troyes the ships were filled almost to overflowing with grain. On the journey home, Genevieve continued to pray for safe passage through dangerous storms and enemy lines. She knew God would bring the fleet and its grains safely home.

Back in Paris, Genevieve had the grain baked into bread. She gave the fresh-baked bread to the poor and the hungry. People were not unkind to Genevieve anymore. They loved and trusted her because she was brave and protected them. Some years later, Paris was again threatened by another army led by Attila the Hun! The Parisian people wanted to run away! But Genevieve asked them to pray and to fast instead. And so the people of Paris trusted good Genevieve, fasting and praying with her as Attila approached closer and closer. In the end, Attila and his army changed directions. Paris was saved!

When Genevieve died, she was buried in the Church of Saints Peter and Paul. Pilgrims came from all over France—other golden-haired girls among them!—crowding together to pray at her tomb. Genevieve continued to do marvelous things for these faithful who came to see her, giving them a small foretaste of the banquet in Heaven. Saint Genevieve is now the Patroness of Paris.

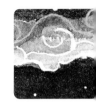

Saint Benedict
(c. 480–547)

SAINT BENEDICT was born in Italy around the year 480. We don't know who his parents were, but he had a twin sister named Scholastica. Their family was probably wealthy because we know they sent Benedict to school not only as a young boy but also up until he was about 20 years old. But when he was 20, Benedict decided he had enough education at school. He wanted to do something different.

FEAST DAY

July
11

Benedict wanted an adventure. He wanted to study in his own way and learn the deeper meaning of life. He left school, and he left home, and he traveled to a lonely wilderness. He found a stream and a lake there, and near the lake he found a cave, a nice one, and he decided to live in the cave. Lucky for him there was a monastery nearby, on top of the hill where the cave was, and one of the monks, Romanus, noticed Benedict and decided to help him.

Romanus kept him supplied with bread and taught him how to pray like the monks did. Benedict loved learning how to pray that way and he practiced very hard. After three years living in his cave, he realized what he wanted to do in life. He decided he wanted to form a new kind of school, a school for holiness, where people could learn how to pray and study how to be closer to God and love Him more. Even though Benedict had spent three years living alone, he thought people could learn holiness better if they lived together and helped each other.

He wrote a plan for his school. It was called *The Rule*, and now we call it *The Rule of Saint Benedict*. He had learned from Romanus how to pray like a monk, so he organized his school to teach people how to pray as the monks did, and he called it a monastery. Everyone at his monastery worked together and prayed together according to a schedule Benedict laid out. There was no talking allowed!—except for praying at Mass and praying at other times. They were silent most of the time, so they could listen to hear God's Word.

Even when they ate dinner together, they did not talk, but one of them read from the Bible or the lives of the saints, and the others listened.

Many, many young men, and older men too, became interested in this school in the wilderness. So many were interested that Benedict had to found more and more monasteries. Women became interested too, and Benedict's twin sister, Scholastica, began to use her brother's *Rule* to make monasteries for women too.

Some people began to be jealous of Benedict because he was so popular, and one of them named Florentius sent him a loaf of bread as a present, only it was poisoned! Benedict was suspicious of the bread. He had a special friend, a raven who lived in the woods but came to see Benedict because Benedict fed him. The raven saw the bread and smelled the poison. He came to see Benedict, maybe to warn him, but Benedict told him not to eat the bread but to carry it far away so no one would be harmed. The raven did as Benedict asked!

In order to help him in his work of founding new monasteries, God gave Benedict a very special gift, the power to work great miracles. Once one of the young monks was crushed when a monastery wall he was helping to build collapsed and killed him. The other monks told Saint Benedict what had happened. He told them to bring the boy's crushed body to him on a blanket. They did, and he told them to put him in his room, and then they left and he closed the door and began to pray. The boy went back to work, restored to life!

Another time a mean, greedy man named Zalla had captured a poor farmer who lived nearby and ordered him to give him all his money, and began to beat him. Trying to find a way to escape, the farmer made up a story that he had given all his money to Saint Benedict. So Zalla tied him up and dragged him to the monastery and burst into Benedict's room where he was reading, demanding the money. Benedict looked up, and noticed that the farmer's hands were tied up. As soon as he looked at the rope, it fell miraculously to the ground and the farmer was free! Zalla was shocked and he promised he would be a better man from then on.

One day, Benedict went to visit his twin sister, Scholastica, whose monastery was nearby. They only visited once a year. She asked Benedict if he could stay longer than usual since they only visited once a year and she missed him, but he refused. Scholastica was disappointed! She prayed to God, and suddenly, according to the story, a thunderstorm began. The rain was pouring down, and Benedict could not leave. God had heard Scholastica's prayer. It was God's way of reminding even someone as holy as Saint Benedict that the greatest miracle of all is love, because God is love, and that he should have listened to his sister because she loved him so much.

Soon after that, three days later, when he was back home in his monastery and in his room, looking out of the window, he suddenly had a vision of his sister's soul leaving her body and going up to Heaven in the form of a dove. He knew then that his sister had died and had been taken to Heaven by God. Now he was glad he had visited with her! And now he knew that she was a saint.

Not long after, Benedict himself died, in 547. So many men and women had been attracted to his monastery schools that *The Rule of Saint Benedict* became the most famous plan for organizing prayer schools in the world. Even today there are many Benedictine monks and nuns who follow *The Rule* in nearly all parts of the world. In 1980, Pope John Paul II made him one of the patron saints of Europe. We remember him on his feast day, July 11.

Blessed Herman *of* Reichenau
(1013–1054)

B LESSED HERMAN was the son of the Count of Altshausen, in Germany. He was born in 1013, with several disabling medical problems. These disabilities meant a life of physical hardships for Herman as he was unable to walk, hardly able to talk, and had a hard time writing. Still, Herman had a charitable heart, taking solace in Our Lady as the Mother of Mercy, and a brilliant intellect which he exercised all his life.

When Herman was 7 years old, his father brought him to the Benedictine monastery at Reichenau, an island in Lake Constance. The monks were able to give Herman the care he needed. Abbot Berno and the other monks loved Herman and helped him get around the monastery by carrying him, and they gave him an excellent education. At the age of 20 Herman entered the Order himself, becoming a Benedictine monk.

Because of his disabilities, Herman spent his life in the monastery on Reichenau Island, dedicating himself to studying. He was bright and his mind was interested in the world around him. He wanted to know more and more about it. He learned to read different languages and wrote books on almost every subject: geometry, astrology, theology, history, music, and poetry. It is these last two subjects that might interest us most because Herman wrote prayers and composed many hymns that we still sing today.

You probably already know his hymns, even if you did not know that Herman wrote them. Herman's hymns include *Come Creator Spirit* (sung at canonizations!), *Kind Mother of the Redeemer* (sung during Advent and Christmas) and *Hail, Holy Queen* (prayed with every Rosary and as the Marian Antiphon for Ordinary Time). Just think, this monk who could barely speak himself has given us some of the most beautiful songs we still sing at church! Herman gave us words for praising God and thanking Mary, while our voices give sound to his prayers even after almost 1000 years.

These beautiful songs arose from Herman's devotion to Our Lady. She comforted him in his great afflictions and physical suffering. His hymns allow us to imagine his deep interior life, speaking to Mary whom he called "Mother of Mercy," "Gate of heaven," "Star of the sea," "Holy Queen," "Our Life," "Our Sweetness," and "Our Hope." He could sing all of this to Mary in his heart because he knew Mary had given us the gospel by becoming Christ's mother. Herman was also letting us know that God is with us even in our sufferings, as Herman himself knew from experience.

The *Salve Regina*, also known as the *Hail Holy Queen*, has a particularly interesting story. The last line of this hymn is "O clement, O loving, O sweet Virgin Mary!" but it wasn't always so. As the story goes, this last line was added to Herman's hymn by Saint Bernard of Clairvaux, but not because he thought he needed to improve Herman's hymn, but because he thought it was so beautiful. As Herman's last line fell silent in the Cathedral, Saint Bernard was so moved that he sang out "O clement, O loving, O sweet Virgin Mary!"

Here are the words of the *Hail Holy Queen* in case you want to sing with Herman too:

> *Hail, Holy Queen, Mother of Mercy, our life, our sweetness and our hope!*
>
> *To thee do we cry, poor banished children of Eve!*
>
> *To thee do we send up our sighs, mourning and weeping in this valley of tears!*
>
> *Turn then, most gracious Advocate, thine eyes of mercy toward us,*
>
> *and after this, our exile, show unto us the blessed fruit of your womb, Jesus!*
>
> *O clement, O loving, O sweet Virgin Mary!*

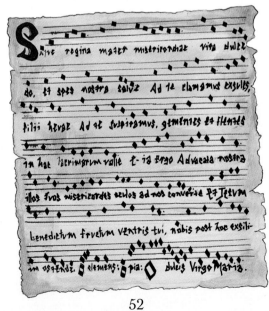

Saint Bernard *of* Clairvaux
(1090–1153)

AINT BERNARD was born in 1090 in Burgundy, France. He and his family lived in a castle! His father, Tescelin, and his brothers were knights. They had armor and horses, shields, swords, and colorful flags they took into battles. Bernard was meant to become a knight, too.

But young Bernard had lots of ideas about what to be when he grew up, and he didn't know which one was right. He loved school and thought he might become a teacher. He loved God and thought he might become a monk. He also thought knights were gallant and brave, and so he thought he might as well be like his father and his brothers. When Bernard was riding to meet his brothers for the siege of Grancey Castle, perhaps thinking about daring deeds as he rode, like scaling castle walls, he decided to stop in a church he found along his way. As he prayed in this church, tears filled his eyes, and it became clear to Bernard that he did not want to be a knight, or a teacher, but a monk. Instead of climbing castle walls in conquest, he would climb the ladder of humility in seeking God.

Bernard turned his sights toward the Abbey of Citeaux, which was not far from his family's castle. The monks there called themselves Cistercians. They lived simply and worked very hard, following *The Rule of Saint Benedict*. They prayed, tended their gardens, and celebrated the Liturgy. Bernard admired their simplicity. He thought it would make it easier to seek God.

But Bernard did not know that just as he was thinking of joining them, the monks were thinking of leaving! These new Cistercians had built their abbey in a swamp, and things were going very badly for them. Imagine their surprise when Bernard showed up with 30 of his friends, his father and brothers, and other relatives to join them! Bernard is nicknamed the Sweet-Tongued Doctor for his ability to persuade others with his words. He had spoken so sweetly of the life of the monk to his friends and family, that they all decided to join him and followed him to Citeaux! Let others scale the walls of castles; we will find God instead!

Bernard continued to speak so sweetly of the monk's life and continued to attract so many new monks, that he was sent out to start another new Cistercian abbey. He was sent to a place called the Valley of Bitterness! But Bernard made it a lovely place where many monks wanted to live. He called it the Valley of Light, or Clairvaux.

As abbot of Clairvaux, Bernard taught his monks how to seek God. He told them they must climb the ladder of humility every day if they want to find God. Bernard was imagining the ladder Jacob saw in a dream coming down from Heaven to Earth (Genesis 28.10-17). Bernard knew God had given us a different kind of ladder by coming down to us in the Incarnation. We can climb this ladder up to God, Bernard said, by first climbing down in humility like God did when He became a little child. Isn't it funny to think about going up by going down?

Saint Bernard also said that Mary is the perfect example of climbing up by climbing down. She was the humble handmaid of the Lord! Just as Bernard praised Mary with Bl. Hermann, we can pray with Saint Bernard to Our Lady. Perhaps you know the *Memorare* prayer. Saint Bernard wrote this prayer (which was a favorite of Saint Teresa of Calcutta!). Maybe we can climb up with Saint Bernard by going down to Mary with this prayer. The *Memorare* goes like this; let's pray it with Saint Bernard:

Remember, O most gracious virgin Mary, that never was it known that anyone who fled to your protection, implored your help, or sought your intercession, was left unaided. Inspired by this confidence, I fly to you, O Virgin of virgins, my mother; to you I come, before you I stand, sinful and sorrowful! O mother of the Word Incarnate, despise not my petitions; but in your mercy hear and answer me. Amen.

Saint Dominic
(1170–1221)

AINT DOMINIC was born in 1170 in Caleruega, Spain, to Felix and Joan Guzman. Before he was even born, Felix and Joan knew their son would do great things for God. Sometimes we are given signs of such things, and Joan believed she had received a sign in a dream. She dreamt that a dog carrying a flaming torch in its mouth leapt from her womb and lit the whole world on fire. This fire-bearing dog was a sign of her son who would zealously teach the truth of the gospel to others. The "fire" of truth is still being spread through the Order of Preachers (or the Dominicans), founded by Saint Dominic in 1216.

After Dominic grew up he traveled all through the lands of Spain, France, and Italy. But he did not travel as you and I travel, in cars or trains or airplanes. Dominic walked. And usually he walked barefoot. Can you imagine walking all around three different countries barefoot? One of Dominic's trips involved walking from Rome (in Italy) to Toulouse (in France), up to Paris (still in France), then down through Spain, around to Milan (back in Italy!), and finally back to Rome. That is 3,380 miles with bare feet! And Dominic would have had to cross the Pyrenees and the Alps, twice.

Just as Joan received signs of Dominic's zeal, 3,380 miles of walking should be a sign for us! Dominic cared very deeply that everyone might understand the truth about the gospel. Why would he care so much about what someone else believes? Because knowing and understanding God changes the whole world—sets it on fire with love! The world, he taught everyone, was created by God, and so the beauty and goodness of all creation tells us about its Creator. First among all these good and beautiful things is the human being, made in God's image and likeness. Dominic knew the Gospels tell us that God "so loved the world, that He gave His only Son" (John 3:16). Dominic wanted everyone to know this Good News, and so Dominic walked 3,380 miles to say so.

Dominic did not walk alone. There were other men out walking and preaching. At first, Dominic joined the others, including several Cistercian monks. At one point, he

crossed paths with Saint Francis of Assisi. When he met Francis, Dominic felt they would be good friends — brothers in preaching love for their Creator. Soon, though, others joined Dominic on his particular journeys, and when there were seven of them, the Pope made them a new religious order: The Order of Preachers. Their job was to preach the Good News all over the world.

One of the ways Dominic and his Preachers taught the faith to so many people in so many places was through the Rosary. The Rosary gave people a very easy way to see the truth of our faith. With the Rosary, Dominic invited everyone to think of God as our Father, Mary as our mother, and Jesus as our Brother.

No matter where in the world he was, Dominic said Mass every day. Once a scholar attending Dominic's Mass noticed a most beautiful smell. Dominic's hands, which had held the Eucharist, smelled more sweetly than any odor the man "had ever experienced in his life." This smell was the "aroma of Christ," a sign given by God of Christ's presence in the Eucharist.

Dominic died in 1221. His body smelled of this same "aroma of Christ" many years after his death. How do we know this? Well, whenever someone is declared a saint in the Catholic Church, their body is moved (we say "translated") from their tomb to a Church for veneration. The bones, or relics, of a saint are holy treasures because they are the "roof" under which Christ entered to dwell with the saint. We could think of relics like an altar after the Mass. Now, when the Dominican brothers went to translate Dominic's relics, they discovered his tomb was so full of "an odor of such sweetness" that it smelled like a whole "storeroom" of perfumes. Dominic's relics and all the earth surrounding his tomb were filled with this "aroma of Christ." One Dominican said, "The fragrance also clung to the hands of the brothers who had touched the relics, so that no matter how often they were washed or rubbed together, the perfume lingered."

Today we pray that Saint Dominic's zeal will linger with us, setting us on fire to know our Creator and Redeemer. Knowing God will reveal the truth about ourselves as God's beloved creation, and the aroma of Christ (2 Cor. 2:15–17). Maybe we will even get to preach the gospel to others all around the world, lighting it "on fire." (Yes, you can take a car or a train or a plane!)

Saint Francis *of* Assisi
(1182–1226)

RANCIS spent Christmas of 1223 in Greccio, an Italian town built right into the rocky edges of a mountainside. On Christmas Eve Francis worked all day, preparing the altar for Midnight Mass. No, not in Greccio's Church, but in a cave-like hollow near Greccio's main square! The cave reminded Francis of the place where Christ was born in Bethlehem, which he had visited on a trip to the Holy Land. Francis set up the altar and then set out to find a donkey, an ox, and lots of hay.

FEAST DAY

October
4

During the Mass, Francis, flanked by the donkey and the ox, wept. But he wasn't sad! No, he was very happy! The joy of Christmas was there for everyone to see, with the Eucharist offered in the middle of this living nativity scene. A soldier in the crowd even professed to seeing a vision of the Christ Child lying in the piled-up hay.

Francis is known for his happy joy. He was always singing and writing songs about Our Lord.

Francis is also known for being very poor. Francis liked being poor because God had become poor in the Incarnation, pouring Himself out for us on the Cross. Because of this, Francis wouldn't even hold a single coin in his hand! But he always made sure the vessels for the Eucharist were made of silver and gold. They were for God, after all, our most priceless Gift!

Perhaps, though, Francis is most famous for his love of Creation. Francis helped worms across roads, freed rabbits from traps, and even tamed a ferocious, man-eating wolf! He preached to fish and birds and to the flowers of the fields. Once he even spoke to a fire, calling it, "Brother Fire." He asked Brother Fire to be "kind and courteous" as a doctor used the fire to fix his failing eyesight. Have you ever talked to a fire? Or a flower? Or a fish?

Many, many years later, a man named G. K. Chesterton said, "Christ is like Saint Francis." He meant that Saint Francis shows us what Christ was like. This was true in a particular way with Saint Francis because he received the stigmata. The stigmata are the five wounds Christ received in His death on the Cross. While in silent prayer in the middle of the night in a place called Mt. La Verna, Saint Francis saw on a Cross a six-winged seraph who looked just like Jesus. When the vision disappeared, Francis had Christ's wounds on his hands, feet, and side. His hands and feet even bore the likeness of the nails! Francis had these stigmata for the rest of his life. He would only let his dearest friend, Brother Leo, help him with the bandages.

Even these wounds were part of Francis's happy joy. With his living nativity he rejoiced at Christmas over Christ's birth. And he shared in Christ's Cross with joy through his stigmata. Francis was happy to be like God Who had become poor by "emptying himself" for us.

Saint Francis died in Assisi in October of 1226. Near the place of his death there is a rose garden where Saint Francis used to talk to the turtle doves. To this day, turtle doves nest in the hands of a statue of Saint Francis placed amongst the roses.

Saint Thomas Aquinas
(1225–1274)

**D**ANGLING IN MID-AIR, THOMAS sees his mother leaning out of the window, watching her son make his escape. Thomas prays desperately, inching his way down the stone wall of the castle tower. Once he hits the ground, he will be off to Paris!

But why is Thomas escaping from his own family's home with the help of his mother?

Well, since he was the youngest son, Thomas's mother and father, Theodora and Landulf d'Aquino, wanted him to become a Benedictine monk at the famous Monte Cassino Abbey. In fact, they had sent him there when he was just 5 years old to begin his studies! They later pulled him out of the Abbey school when it was invaded by warring soldiers, and Thomas continued his studies in Naples, where he met a Dominican preacher. The Dominican Order was still new, having been founded by Saint Dominic only in 1216. Saint Dominic had wandered the Spanish, French, and Italian countryside preaching the Gospel so that people would know the Truth.

Inspired by the Dominicans in Naples, Thomas decided he wanted to study in Paris and become a Dominican friar. But his family still wanted him to become a Benedictine. And so they locked him in the tower of the family castle at Roccasecca. Eventually, Theodora came to feel sorry for her son and helped him escape. And that is how we find Thomas Aquinas, dangling from his window, making a daring escape from his own home!

Once free, Thomas made his way to Paris, where he studied under Saint Albert the Great, and where Saint Bonaventure was his classmate. However, Thomas's tower descent was not the last time he was found hovering mid-air. When Thomas would say Mass, he would often levitate, hovering above the ground before the altar!

Thomas eventually became a professor himself. He loved to learn about God, which seemed a wondrously endless task, and to share what he learned with others. He loved books so much that he even described Our Lord as a Book. Christ, Thomas said, is the

Book of Charity. We read about God's love in Christ's humanity. We learn about God's love for us in the way that Christ, as God, was tired and hungry and sad and worried, just like we are. Thomas also said that Christ can write on our hearts, as He did with Saint Ignatius. Not with a pen or a pencil, but with His words of love. In this way, as the Church, we become pages in Christ's Book of Charity. With Christ's help, we can teach others about God. This is the Dominican Way!

However, one day, while Thomas was celebrating Mass, he had one of his ecstatic visions that sometimes made him levitate. He never told us what he saw. But whatever it was, it made him stop writing books. And he was in the middle of his greatest and longest book yet (the *Summa Theologica*). He did tell us that all he had written suddenly seemed like "straw" compared to what he saw of God's love while celebrating the Eucharist. There are things so beautiful about God that even the best teachers cannot put them into words! The words, we could imagine, sort of dangle between Heaven and Earth. How would you describe the most beautiful thing you have ever, ever seen?

Thomas died soon after this vision, in 1274. Today many people still read Thomas's books, hoping to see some of the beautiful things about God that were written by God on Thomas's heart and so in his books.

Saint Catherine *of* Siena
(1347–1380)

AINT CATHERINE was born on the Feast of the Annunciation (March 25) in 1347, in a town called Siena, which is in the beautiful hills of the central part of Italy. She was the 25th of 25 children born to her mother, whose name was Lapa, and her father, whose name was Jacopo.

When Saint Catherine was 7 years old she had a beautiful vision while she was walking with one of her brothers in Siena. She looked up and saw the Lord Himself, and Saints Peter, Paul, and John. The Lord smiled at her and blessed her with His hand. Her brother did not see the Lord, but he did see a brilliant light. Saint Catherine decided that her vision meant the Lord wanted her to talk to Him often by praying frequently, and she decided to be a prayerful person for the rest of her life.

When Saint Catherine was 16 years old, she decided to join the Dominican sisters, but not the kind that live in a convent. She joined the Third Order Dominicans who lived in their own homes instead of a convent but wore the Dominican habit, which is a white dress with a black cloak. They spent time together praying and helping the sick and the needy in the city. Catherine was the youngest member of the group, and she still spent most of her time at home with her family. She helped her family with chores, especially her mother, who had so many people to take care of. Her brothers helped her father in their business, which was dyeing wool with beautiful colors so it could be woven into threads and used to make clothes. Catherine prayed in her own room when it was quiet.

Catherine had a generous heart and she shared her family's food and money with poor people who knocked on their door. Her generous heart led her to begin to work in the hospitals with the sick people that no one else wanted to work with because they were disfigured or contagious or yelled and cursed at people. Catherine knew they were lonely and afraid. One woman had leprosy. She was mean and cursed Catherine and yelled at her, but Catherine just took care of her calmly. Her kindness converted the woman, who

died in Catherine's arms. Unfortunately, Catherine began to have leprosy herself. But she still washed and buried the woman. After the woman was buried, Catherine noticed that her own hands and arms were healed of leprosy by a miracle.

Another woman, named Andrea, had cancer and had a deep sore that smelled so terrible that no one would even enter the room. Some people vomited when they smelled it. Catherine's generous heart led her to take care of this woman, washing the sore and changing the bandages, until Andrea died. Catherine had a vision of the Lord with the blood pouring out of His wounds. She knew that He was telling her that by taking care of this woman, which was a difficult act of loving kindness, she was coming to understand more and more how the Lord loves us with His own blood, and even when our sins might make our souls "smelly" He still takes care of us.

Catherine was then led to another beautiful act of kindness. She befriended a young man who had been unjustly condemned to death. She became his friend. She comforted him and prayed with him and even walked with him to his execution and held his head between her hands so that when it was cut off it would not fall to the ground. This man's soul went straight to Heaven, carried there by the love of his friend, Catherine.

All of these acts of love gave Catherine the courage to speak to important people who were making terrible mistakes, because she knew that when she was telling them to reform and make better decisions, she would be saying it out of love. She wrote to princes and to queens and most famously she visited the Pope, who at that time had left the city of Rome, where he belonged, and was living in France, where he did not belong. She spoke bravely to him, but with love (instead of calling him "your Holiness" or "holy Father" she called him "Dad"!), and he listened! He went back to Rome.

Saint Catherine received Holy Communion every day of her life. Receiving Holy Communion was the most beautiful part of her day. She knew that in Holy Communion she was receiving into her heart the love of the Lord Jesus and that she would be able to share that love for the rest of the day with anyone who needed it, whether it was the woman Andrea or the Pope, or her mother, or her friends, or anyone else. When her father died, Catherine prayed that his soul would go straight to heaven, and she was granted a vision of him entering heaven in response!

Saint Catherine died on April 28, 1380, when she was only 33 — the same age as Jesus when He died. This was a sign that she had followed the Lord so closely in her life that she resembled Him in her love for everyone around her. Her body was buried near a special Church in Rome, the Basilica of Santa Maria Sopra Minerva, near the Pantheon, which is one of the oldest churches in Rome. When many miracles were reported to have occurred after people prayed to her, they transferred her body to rest inside the Basilica. Some of her relics, however, were brought back to Siena, where she was born. Her mother, Lapa, was still alive at the time and carried them into the Basilica of Saint Dominic in Siena.

Saint Joan *of* Arc
(1412–1431)

FEAST DAY

May
30

AINT THÉRÈSE OF LISIEUX loved Saint Joan of Arc. She loved her for many reasons, as we all do, but one of the most simple was this: in French, Joan's name is "Jeanne." Pronouncing this name properly in French, one cannot help but smile when saying "Jeanne." A smile is simply the way the mouth naturally moves—try it! For Saint Thérèse, a smile is a prayer. So, even just to say the name of this saint, "Jeanne," is a happy and prayerful thing! But Joan is many people's favorite saint, especially soldiers and the French people. After all, she is a patron saint of France!

The d'Arc family lived in Domremy, France, right next to the parish Church. The d'Arcs were peasants, and so as a young girl Joan helped with the farm. She especially liked to spin, to sew, and to look after the sheep. The meadows around her home rolled across the landscape, lush and deeply green. The fresh, clear waters of the Meuse River meandered by, winding their playful way through the sheep's pasture. Joan would sit nearby, spinning or weaving crowns of flowers for the parish statue of the Virgin Mary, and praying to "Our Father, who art in Heaven."

But not so far away, life was much less peaceful. France and England had been at war for almost 100 years! Outside the battles, England burned the farm fields of France. Thus, generation after generation were not only dying in battles, but they were also so very hungry. The situation seemed almost entirely hopeless for France. When Joan was in the fields with her sheep, she was quick to give her food to hungry children wandering the countryside.

One day, when Joan was 13, she was working in her father's garden when she heard a Voice calling to her. The Voice first came from the direction of the parish church, accompanied by a great light. Joan was afraid at the beginning, but she continued to hear this Voice speaking to her wherever she would go. She came to recognize the Voice as that

of the Archangel Michael. Michael said to her, "Go, raise the siege which is being made before the City of Orleans. Go!" Michael was joined by Saint Margaret of Antioch and Saint Catherine of Alexandria, who also spoke to Joan, urging her to lead France in battle. The first time Joan saw Michael, Margaret, and Catherine, she wept because "they were so beautiful." Joan heard the Voice of Michael and saw these visions for several years before she could convince others to give her arms and to let her lead France.

The *voices* of these saints continued to guide and to guard Joan. They helped her speak to the King of France and to war-worn French generals. They helped this peasant girl lead soldiers and execute brilliant military campaigns, though she did not even know how to read and write.

Joan was given a special white suit of armor, a sword, a strong black horse, and a military standard—or a military flag—bearing the names "Jesus" and "Mary." Joan loved her standard because it bore those two names. And so young Joan, barely 18 years old, led the armies of France into battle after battle. And she won! Battle after battle!

But Joan, who, under her suit of armor, was still just a sweet, young peasant girl, did not want to kill anyone. In fact, she never did, not even in the heaviest battles she fought. Though she had a sword, she never carried it in battle. She only carried her beloved standard, the names of "Mary" and "Jesus" flying high above her black horse and her white armor. After battle, Joan would tend the wounded and comfort the dying. It was not unusual to find Joan crying, an enemy soldier in her lap, as Joan held him until his last breath.

Joan's greatest victory was the Siege of Orleans, as St. Michael had foretold. After that battle, she was called the Maid of Orleans, or La Pucelle. The victory opened her way to march on Reims. All along her way to Reims, the English troops surrendered without a fight. In Reims Joan herself crowned Charles VII, King of France!

Joan believed her job was done. She asked to go home to her mother and father. She truly was but a girl who loved her home, her farm, and her parish church. She wanted to tend her sheep by the Meuse River, weave Mary's flower crowns, and go to Mass.

Joan would not get her wish. While protecting the city of Compiegne, she was pulled from her horse by an English archer. Joan of Arc was captured!

Joan was put in jail and heavily guarded. Still she tried to escape; once by jumping out her window, which was 70 feet off the ground! Tired of these attempts, her guards put her in chains and an iron cage. She defended herself, saying "the prisoner has a right to escape!"

Soon Joan was put on trial. Joan, who could not read or write, was brought to court before dozens and dozens of learned men, all trying to trick her. The English had become so afraid of her military genius that the court tried everything. They accused her of heresy. They accused her of witchcraft. They accused her of lying. The court was cruel, and though Joan spoke honestly and truly, and with a clarity none of the dozens of learned men possessed, they betrayed her and condemned her to death.

Joan of Arc was burned at the stake in Rouen on May 30, 1431. Sweet, brave Joan prayed to Jesus from the flames, asking a bystander to hold a crucifix before her eyes. The executioner himself was moved by Joan's purity and courage. He tells us that he could not reduce her heart to ashes, no matter how he tried.

And so Joan's testimony of love remains. Like our Lord, she went to her death abandoned and sad, but loving all mankind anyway. That is why, even today, so many love Joan of Arc. We can smile and say, "Jeanne, pray for us!" And we know we have a courageous friend who will tend our wounds and love us enough to fight to bring us to God in Heaven.

Saint Juan Diego
(1474–1548)

AINT JUAN DIEGO was born in Cuauhtitlan. His family was part of the Chichimeca Indian Tribe in the land we call Mexico. His parents named him Cuauhtlatoa, or "Talking Eagle." "Talking Eagle" was baptized by the first Franciscan missionaries in Mexico when he was about 50 years old. At his Baptism, "Talking Eagle" took the name Juan Diego.

December 9, 1531, was a Saturday. That morning Juan Diego was walking to the Church of Saint James in Tlatelolco for catechism class, crossing Tepeyac Hill. Something very beautiful happened to Juan Diego that Saturday morning on Tepeyac Hill—a sort of catechism class he never expected!

The earliest accounts of Juan Diego's experience that Saturday morning tell us that as he neared Tepeyac Hill, he heard beautiful singing, as if different precious birds were singing and as if the hill were answering them in song. "Their songs were most pleasant and very enjoyable, better than that of the coyoltotol or of tzinitzcan or of the other precious birds." Juan Diego thought maybe he was dreaming or maybe he was in Heaven. He wanted to see where this beautiful music was coming from, up on Tepeyac Hill. Then, he heard someone calling to him: "Juan, dearest, dignified Juan Diego!" How strange and wonderful! He decided to climb the hill to have a look!

When Juan Diego reached the top of the hill, he saw Our Lady! It was Mary who had called him! She called him to her side. Approaching her, "he marveled greatly at her perfect beauty. Her clothing appeared like the sun, and it gave forth rays." The cliff where she was standing received her radiance "like arrows of light." Everything looked like precious jewels, glowing "with the splendors of the rainbow." "Even the thorns" of the cacti "sparkled like gold!" Juan Diego bowed low and waited for Our Lady to speak.

She asked Juan Diego to do a special task for her—to have a "house" built for her on Tepeyac Hill so that she might, like a Mother, care for her children. This is what she said:

Know and be certain in your heart, my most abandoned son, that I am the Ever-Virgin Holy Mary, Mother of God, of the One through Whom We Live, the Creator of Persons, the Owner of What is Near and Together, of the Lord of Heaven and Earth. I very much want and ardently desire that my hermitage be erected in this place. In it I will show and give to all people all my love, my compassion, my help, and my protection, because I am your merciful mother and the mother of all the nations that live on this earth who would love me, who would speak with me, who would search for me, and who would place their confidence in me. There I will hear their laments and remedy and cure all their miseries, misfortunes, and sorrows.

Moved by this Mother's compassion, Juan Diego went straight to ask Bishop Zumarraga to build a home for Mary. The people needed their Mother! But the Bishop did not believe Juan Diego and sent him away. Juan Diego immediately returned to Tepeyac Hill with the disappointing news for Our Lady. He felt struck down and discouraged, and so he asked her to entrust someone more important or well-known with her message. Still, Our Lady insisted: "It must be you, Juan Diego!" Juan Diego and only Juan Diego could help realize her desire for the Church to be built near Tepeyac Hill.

And so he tried again. This time the Bishop asked that Juan Diego return a third time, and with a sign.

Our Lady promised this sign to Juan Diego if he returned to Tepeyac Hill the following morning, the 12th of December. But the next morning Juan Diego avoided Tepeyac Hill. His uncle, Juan Bernardino, had become gravely ill in the night. Juan Diego needed to find the parish priest to give his uncle the Last Rites and quickly, even if it meant he could not meet the marvelous and sun-soaked Lady as he had promised.

Yet, she made sure to meet Juan Diego! She went down to meet him at the edge of Tepeyac Hill as he passed by. Seeing Juan Diego's distress, she assured him that his uncle would be healed. In fact, she had appeared to Juan Bernardino that same morning to heal him, telling him that she was the ever-virgin Holy Mary of Guadalupe! She was already

giving them the compassion and love of a mother. Her next words to Juan Diego were very beautiful and remain very famous: "Let not your heart be troubled. Do not fear that sickness, nor any other sickness or anxiety. Am I not here, your Mother?"

Then, to accomplish the sign promised, Our Lady asked Juan Diego to climb Tepeyac Hill, to pick all the flowers he found blooming there, and to bring them to her. Juan Diego was astonished to find an abundance of beautiful Castilian flowers, "open and flowering." Remember, it was the middle of December! The middle of winter! The flowers "were very fragrant, as if they were filled with fine pearls, filled with the morning dew." Our Lady arranged the roses in Juan Diego's tilma, or cloak, and sent him to Bishop Zumarraga. All along his way Juan Diego enjoyed "the scent of the beautiful flowers."

Juan Diego waited a long time for the Bishop to see him. All day and into the night! When Bishop Zumarraga finally admitted Juan Diego, Juan Diego fell on his knees and said:

> "The Lady from heaven, Holy Mary, precious Mother of God," she "accepted willingly what you asked for, a sign and a proof so that her desire and will may come about." "She sent me to the top of the hill, where I had seen her before, so that I might cut the flowers from Castile. After I had cut them, I took them to the bottom of the hill. And she, with her precious little hands, took them; she arranged them in the hollow of my mantle, so that I might bring them to you, and deliver them personally."

Juan Diego then let go of his tilma and the Castilian flowers cascaded out, uncovering an image of Our Lady, Holy Mary of Guadalupe! The bishop fell to his knees, and the building of the church began soon after this Tuesday meeting. Juan Diego's tilma bearing Our Lady of Guadalupe's image was placed in the church, where her children could visit with their Mother. Even today, when Pope Francis made a pilgrimage to Mexico City, he said he was going "to visit" with his Mother and "to look into her eyes." Juan Diego, Our Lady's most humble son, spent the rest of his life as a hermit in a hut on Tepeyac Hill, close to his Mother. He died in 1548.

Saint Rose *of* Lima
(1586–1617)

AINT ROSE OF LIMA was born on April 20, 1586. Her father was named Gaspar Flores. He was a soldier. His wife, Rose's mother, was named Maria. She was part Inca. They were very happily married, and they had 13 children together. We know some of Rose's brothers' and sisters' names: Bernadine and Juana (sisters) and Francisco, Antonio, Gaspar, and Andrés (brothers).

As Saint Rose was growing up, she loved to work in her family's garden, where she liked to grow flowers most of all. She also learned to sew. She especially loved to create beautiful, embroidered patterns with many colors of thread, including designs full of flowers and birds. Sometimes when she was in the garden, she hummed duets (she used to say) with the locusts or the bees in the flowers and trees.

When she was very young, she also learned about Saint Catherine of Siena from reading about her life. She decided right then and there she wanted to be just like Saint Catherine, so she taught herself, little by little, to pray. She could walk to the chapel near her house and go to Mass and pray in adoration before the Blessed Sacrament. She began to receive Holy Communion every day (which was very unusual at that time). She also gave up fruit for Lent and then for the whole year, and, even though she was not old enough to have to fast for Lent, she still did, and she kept that up all year too, just like Saint Catherine.

One of her brothers helped her build a little cottage or hut in her family's garden and she began to spend most of her time there, even at night, because she liked to be alone to pray. She was a living Rose in the family garden! Her parents hoped she would marry a nice young man from Lima, but she had studied the life of prayer for so long, even as a teenager, that she preferred to continue to study how to pray and to learn more and more. This captured all of her interest, so that she was not interested in going out very much, except to church, or in meeting the men her parents hoped she would marry.

But she did make friends. Her closest friend was also a saint, Martin de Porres, who was an indigenous boy just a little older than she was (he was 15 when they met). He had already decided to spend his life studying the life of prayer and helping the poor captured Africans who were sold mercilessly as slaves. Rose learned from her friend how to find the poor and to help them. She knew Saint Catherine had taken care of the poor, too.

Also like her spiritual friend Saint Catherine of Siena, Rose joined the Third Order of Dominicans. That means she did not become a nun, but she lived at home and wore the Dominican habit and learned to pray as the Dominicans pray.

When she was in her 20's, her family lost nearly all their money. Saint Rose took over the garden and grew the most beautiful flowers in the city. She sold them at the market. She also began to sew for the rich ladies of Lima, making lace for them and embroidering their dresses and anything else they wanted. She gave her parents most of the money she earned.

But she also asked her brother to help her build another little room onto her hut in the garden, and she began to take in poor people who were sick or needed help. She used some of her money to help them. Her friend Martin de Porres probably spread the news that helpless people who needed assistance could ask Saint Rose to help them.

Rose worked during the day after Mass in the morning, and she spent most of the night working on her other love, praying more and more in silence. The Lord revealed many secrets to Rose without words. She also said she had visions of the devil. He tried to scare her terribly and make her stop praying. But she told him to go away and not to bother her. She also liked to play spiritual games. She told Martin and his friends that she would say 12 rosaries (one for each member of her family, for instance), and they would see if they could beat her. We don't know who won.

Some people laughed at Saint Rose and made fun of her for living differently from other people, but she just prayed for them. She decided to wear a crown of thorns, to remind her of the sufferings of Jesus and of the sorrowful mysteries of the rosary, but on top she placed roses so no one knew what was underneath. She seemed always to be wearing only a crown of roses.

Like Saint Catherine, she died very young, on August 24, 1617. She was only 31. When the news spread that she had died, all the people she had helped and all their friends and all the people who had asked her to pray for them started to gather around her family's house. Pretty soon there was a big crowd.

When it came time for her funeral, it took three days to carry her body from her house to the church. So many people loved her dearly. She had been kind to anyone who met her, even those who laughed at her. People were proud to have a neighbor like Saint Rose. They all wanted to say good-bye and to touch her casket and to ask for her prayers in Heaven. Finally, even the mayor of the city and other city officials came to help carry the body into the church. Many miracles were reliably reported after her death. In Peru she is still so beloved that her picture is on Peruvian money, on the highest banknote (like our $100 bill)! Saint Rose's feast day is August 23.

Saints Zélie & Louis Martin
(1831–1877 | 1823–1894)

ÉLIE'S name before she was married was Zélie Guérin. She had an older sister and a younger brother growing up. Her dad was named Isidore. She went to a beautiful school run by Sisters, who were named the Religious of the Sacred Hearts of Jesus and Mary and of the Perpetual Adoration of the Blessed Sacrament. That is a long name! She loved her school, and the Sisters helped her think about what she wanted to do in life.

FEAST DAY

July

12

She decided that she wanted to be a Sister like they were. But when she applied to be a Sister (in a different place, not at her school), she was not accepted. She was disappointed but she decided that that meant God wanted her to do something else. So she started out by learning to make lace. Lace is very difficult to make! You have to concentrate and you have to be very good with your fingers and a needle. Zélie became one of the most famous lacemakers in France. She loved to sit at her front window and sew lace in the sunlight that came through the window, and to listen to the birds outside.

Guess how she met the man that she wanted to marry? She met him by chance while walking across a long bridge in their town. He was walking the other way, and she knew by that one brief meeting that she wanted to marry him. Isn't that amazing? It is also very beautiful. His name was Louis Martin.

Louis must have had the same idea, because his mom, Marie-Anne-Fanny, arranged for her son to meet Zélie. Three months later they were married, on Tuesday, July 13, 1858. They were married at midnight! Imagine having a wedding in the middle of the night! But at that time, this was a common way to get married. It was nice for them, because they were able to spend their wedding night in their new home, instead of going on a long trip.

Louis was a watchmaker. Like lace, watches are very difficult to make! You have to concentrate and be very good with your fingers as you put tiny gears together to make

the watch work. Louis also loved the outdoors, going fishing, and traveling. Big clouds, thunderstorms, and the ocean were some of his favorite things. When he and Zélie had their children, he would take his girls on picnics in big meadows full of flowers, on trips to the seashore, and on pilgrimages. Once they went all the way to Rome and spoke to the Pope!

Louis and Zélie both had a workshop in their new home. Zélie continued to sew lace, and Louis made watches. Zélie wrote a letter to one of her daughters telling her how happy she and Louis were to have children, and how much joy it gave her. Their most famous child, Thérèse, was their ninth. She was born in the middle of winter, on January 2, 1873. She, and four of her sisters, eventually became nuns. All of the sisters had happy memories of their childhood and of their parents. One of them, whose name was Pauline, said, in later years after both Zélie and Louis had died, "My parents always seemed to me to be saints. We [children] were filled with respect and admiration for them. Sometimes I asked myself if there could be others like them on earth. I never saw any such around me." That's a very beautiful memory to have of your parents!

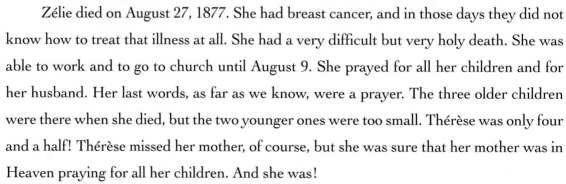

Zélie died on August 27, 1877. She had breast cancer, and in those days they did not know how to treat that illness at all. She had a very difficult but very holy death. She was able to work and to go to church until August 9. She prayed for all her children and for her husband. Her last words, as far as we know, were a prayer. The three older children were there when she died, but the two younger ones were too small. Thérèse was only four and a half! Thérèse missed her mother, of course, but she was sure that her mother was in Heaven praying for all her children. And she was!

Louis died on July 29, 1894, after a long illness. Before he died, he assured his daughters that they would see each other again in Heaven.

The Church decided that Zélie and her husband, Louis, were deserving to be remembered as saints, and they were declared to be saints (we say, "canonized") on October 8, 2015. Their feast day is July 12, the day before their wedding anniversary.

Saint Bernadette
(1844–1879)

BERNADETTE SOUBIROUS was born in Lourdes, France, on January 7, 1844. She was the oldest of François and Louise Soubirous' nine children. Bernadette was quite sick with asthma even as a little girl. It was often hard for her to breathe. And her health was not helped by the fact that her family was so poor that they lived in the old town jail! François had been a miller, but when the brook ran dry, the family had to move and François had to find different work. Their new one-room home in the jail had two beds, a table with chairs, and a fireplace. The windows were barred just as when it was a jail!

One cold, clear February day when Bernadette was 14, her mother sent her to collect firewood in the nearby Sallet Woods. Her sister, Marie, and their school friend, Jeanne, went with her. They walked through the woods, along the Gave River, and over the rocks of the Massabielle Grotto. This Grotto was a scary place! Pigs sheltered there during thunderstorms. The townspeople used it as a dump. And the children of Lourdes told many ghost stories about Massabielle. But on that cold, clear February day something wonderful and unexpected happened at the Massabielle Grotto.

Bernadette was sitting there alone. Marie and Jeanne had hurried ahead of her, crossing through the icy stream to find more firewood. Bernadette was busy taking off her shoes and socks when the wind suddenly started blowing without moving any of the trees! Then a beautiful woman appeared in the Grotto, luminous like the sun. Bernadette rubbed her eyes again and again. Was she really seeing such a wonderfully beautiful Lady? Yes, she was!

Bernadette remembered meeting Our Lady this way:

I heard a noise like a sudden gust of wind. When I turned my head toward the prairie, I saw that the trees were not swaying at all, so I began removing my stockings again. I heard the same noise again. When I raised my head and looked at the Grotto, I saw a Lady in white. She was wearing a white gown with a blue sash, a white veil and a golden rose on each foot, the same color as the chain of her Rosary, which had white beads. She was surrounded with white light, but it was not a blinding light. She had blue eyes. When I first saw her, I was a little bit afraid. Thinking that what I was seeing was an illusion, I rubbed my eyes, but it made no difference: I still saw the same Lady. So I put my hand in my pocket and took out my Rosary. I tried in vain to make the sign of the cross; I was not able to raise my hand to my forehead. When I realized this, I froze completely in fear. The Lady took the Rosary she was holding between her hands and she made the sign of the cross. Then I tried a second time and this time I was able to do it. Immediately after I had made the sign of the cross, the great fear that had seized me disappeared. I knelt and prayed the Rosary, in the presence of this beautiful Lady. She passed the beads of her Rosary between her fingers, but she did not move her lips. When I finished praying the Rosary, she made a sign to me to draw near to her, but I did not dare. Then she suddenly disappeared.

Our Lady visited Bernadette 17 more times at the Massabielle Grotto. They became good friends. Bernadette knew that Our Lady loved her very much. During one of these visits the Lady asked Bernadette to dig up a spring for everyone to drink from and to wash in. Bernadette dug in the dirt with her bare hands. But all she found at first was a bit of muddy water. She followed Our Lady's instructions and drank the muddy water and even washed her face in it! Today the spring at the Grotto flows with clear, miraculous water. Pilgrims from all over the world travel to Lourdes to drink the water and wash in it. Sometimes they are miraculously healed of sickness and sadness.

On their last visit together, The Lady revealed her name to Bernadette. She said, "I am the Immaculate Conception." But she said it to Bernadette in the language Bernadette herself spoke: *"Qué soy era immaculada councepcioũ."* This beautiful woman truly was Our Lady, the Virgin Mary, come down to little Bernadette.

Bernadette's love for Mary and Jesus grew her whole life. Eventually, she left Lourdes to be a nun in Nevers, another town in France. Bernadette joined the Sisters of Charity and Christian Instruction and became Sister Marie-Bernard. Her order ran schools and hospitals. In Nevers, she nursed the sick, but she also grew more and more sick herself. Bernadette had tuberculosis.

Bernadette called her bed in the infirmary her "little white chapel." The sisters draped a white canopy over her bed for privacy, and Bernadette pinned holy cards all over the canopy so she could continue to gaze on Our Lady, Her Son, and the saints.

Bernadette missed home very much. She was always writing letters to her family and friends. Most of her letters ended with these words, "I close with an affectionate kiss," and because she could not return home to Lourdes: "[I] will meet you in the Sacred Hearts of Jesus and Mary." Bernadette died on April 16, 1879, in her little white chapel in Nevers, France. Her last words were the names of Jesus, Mary, and Joseph, whom she had longed to be with ever since that cold February day at Massabielle when Our Lady first greeted her.

Venerable Augustus Tolton
(1854–1897)

AUGUSTUS JOHN TOLTON was born into slavery in Missouri on April 1, 1854. He and his family worked on the Eliot and Hager Plantations, where they were also baptized. When the Civil War broke out, Augustus's father, Peter Paul Tolton, escaped on the Underground Railroad to fight for his family's freedom in the Union Army. Peter Tolton died as a Union soldier.

Soon after Peter Paul escaped, Augustus's mother, Martha Jane, took nine-year-old Augustus and his siblings, Charley and Anne, and fled into the night. If they could cross the Mississippi River, they would be free! But the way was not easy.

First, they crossed 20 miles of rough fields and forest on foot. They had to be very brave! The miles to the river were full of bounty hunters looking for runaway slaves. During the day, they hid.

Then they had to cross the wide and swift Mississippi River. The free state of Illinois lay just on the other side. Union Soldiers helped them cross in a rickety old rowboat with just one oar. They paddled and prayed, paddled and prayed, and finally reached shore near Quincy, Illinois. Martha Jane and her children were free!

But freedom did not mean everything was easy for the Tolton family. They would continually meet people who looked unkindly upon them for their skin color. Sometimes life felt like a raging river or a stormy sea!

Martha Jane taught her children about God by singing spirituals. By Martha Jane's example, the Church became Augustus's "boat." The disciples had once rowed on the stormy Sea of Galilee, and Christ was there to say, "Peace!" In the boat of the Church, this would be Augustus's message, too.

The Toltons settled in Quincy, where Martha Jane, Augustus, and Charley worked in a cigar factory. They also joined Saint Boniface Parish, though they quickly found the waters there stormy, as parishioners were unwelcoming of them because of their race. They moved to Saint Lawrence Parish instead.

At Saint Lawrence Parish, Augustus met a good priest named Fr. McGirr. Aside from Martha Jane, Father McGirr became Augustus's greatest champion: he taught him how to be an altar server, helped him go to school, and, noticing Augustus's great fervor in prayer and altar service, asked Augustus if he would like to become a priest. He would! Augustus became the first black Catholic priest in America!

But the way was not easy. The waters were often stormy for Augustus: no seminary in America would accept a black student. So Augustus studied in Rome instead, at the College of the Propagation of the Faith. He sailed across the Atlantic Ocean to study with seminarians from all around the world. In Rome Augustus found himself among students of many different skin colors. Studying to be priests together, they lived Christ's word of "Peace!"

Augustus was ordained in 1886 at the age of 31, and was then sent home to be the pastor of Saint Joseph's parish in Quincy, Illinois. His new parishioners loved his preaching and his beautiful singing voice. It seemed Fr. Augustus had brought Christ's word of "Peace!" home.

But, before long, new storms brewed! Fellow priests grew jealous of "good Fr. Gus" and his happy parish. Poorly treated by them, Fr. Augustus asked to be moved.

In 1889 Fr. Augustus moved to Chicago with Martha Jane. A number of his parishioners also moved from Quincy to Chicago with them. With Martha Jane's support, Augustus worked hard to build the first Black National Catholic Parish, which was named for Saint Monica. Saint Katharine Drexel even sent them money for their new church building: $36,000, which is like sending someone a million dollars today! Saint Monica's was eventually built at the corner of 36th and Dearborn Streets on the South Side of Chicago. When Fr. Augustus arrived in Chicago, he had just 30 parishioners, but he would soon have 600, both black and white.

But Fr. Augustus did not think of it in this way. He simply thought he had *Catholic* parishioners, all passengers on Christ's boat. There, through the Eucharist offered by Fr. Augustus, Christ spoke the words of peace. The parishioners became brothers and sisters in God's love, poured out for each and every one of them. Together they "paddled" and prayed.

Fr. Augustus died in July of 1897 during a severe heat wave in Chicago. Walking home from the train station in 105-degree weather, he collapsed on the sidewalk. The journey of his life was over, but we can still find "good Fr. Gus" at the helm, saying, "Peace!"

Saint Thérèse *of* Lisieux
(1873–1897)

SAINT THÉRÈSE is busier now than ever. She spends her Heaven doing good on Earth, just as she promised she would. Saint Thérèse forecast these good deeds, describing them as a "shower of roses." Still today, she answers prayers, and these answers are often accompanied by roses or by the fragrance of roses! The prayers she answers are both big and small.

Saint Thérèse herself was always busy praying. She prayed for big things and small things when she was growing up. When she was very young, she prayed for her mother, who was dying of cancer. Then she prayed not to be so very sad after she died. She prayed for the poor people in her town. Once she prayed for a man she read about in the newspaper: he was to be executed, and she hoped he might turn to God before his death. (He did!) She prayed that she might become a Carmelite nun, like her sisters, even though she was just 14. And then, as a nun, she prayed that she might learn to love everyone around her, even those who annoyed her.

And so Saint Thérèse came to know a lot about prayer. She knew that even a smile is a prayer. She knew prayer builds a friendship with God. She knew her life needed to be a prayer. This way, she could love everyone around her, even when they were annoying, because she would be so immersed in her friendship with God that she could love them like God loves them.

Saint Thérèse knew how God loves. She often felt loved by God in many big and little ways. About the day she joined the sisters at Carmel, she wrote: "That January day, the weather was so mild, snow seemed unlikely. However, upon returning to the cloister, the first thing that struck my eye was the statue of 'the little Jesus' smiling at me from the midst of flowers and lights. Immediately afterwards my glance was drawn to the snow: the monastery garden was white like me! What thoughtfulness on the part of Jesus! Anticipating the desires of his fiancée, He gave her snow. Snow! What mortal

bridegroom, no matter how powerful he may be, could make snow fall from heaven to charm his beloved?"

For most of her life, Saint Thérèse desired to do big things for God, and lots of them. She wanted to be a warrior, a priest, an apostle, a doctor of the Church, and a martyr. "My Jesus," she said, "fling open the book in which are set down the deeds of every saint. I want to perform them all for you!" And, in a way, she did, because she did all things with love. She kept herself busy with all kinds of household chores: laundry, ironing, cleaning, cooking meals, working in the sacristy or in the garden, and caring for the elderly and the sick.

Thérèse was able to stay so busy because she learned, through prayer, that God does not demand big deeds. He only asks for love. He once said, "Just as I have loved you, you also should love one another" (John 13:34). And so Thérèse kept herself busy, doing every little thing for her sisters. "Love is not something that stays shut up in one's heart," she said; we should show it to "all those who are of the household," in every little way.

These little acts of love are what we call today Thérèse's "Little Way." Thérèse learned this "Little Way" from her parents, Saints Louis and Zélie Martin. Thérèse's childhood home was always busy with loving! Her sisters call Thérèse the "Apostle of the Little Way" because she revealed her family's great but small ways of loving God to the whole world.

Saint Thérèse died on the 30th of September in 1897. She was just 24. Her Carmelite sisters tell us that it was a rainy day, but, despite this, the birds sang outside Thérèse's window with all their might until she died that evening. What a choir! When she died the rain clouds quickly dispersed and the stars shone in a bright, clear sky. Perhaps this was so we could begin to look for Thérèse's shower of roses!

Blessed Pier Giorgio Frassati
(1901–1925)

P IER GIORGIO was born into the wealthy Frassati family of Turin, Italy, on April 6, 1901. It was Holy Saturday. His father, Alfredo, was a politician and owner of a newspaper called *La Stampa*. His mother, Adelaide, was a celebrated painter. Pier Giorgio had one sister, with whom he was very close. Her name was Luciana.

FEAST DAY

July

4

Pier Giorgio loved the sea and the mountains. In summertime, he went boating or swimming in the sea. He also liked to ride his bike, and he would bike ride in the mountains for three and four hours at a time. He enjoyed climbing the mountains most, and he would scale rocky cliffs to reach the top. Of winter skiing trips, Pier Giorgio once said, they "are like eating cherries: once you start you cannot stop."

When Pier Giorgio was 17 he joined Turin's Saint Vincent de Paul Society. This decision gave his life a definitive direction: "to follow the way of the Cross." From then on, he visited the homes of the poor on Fridays. He would give his whole allowance to the poor in secret, even his daily bus fare. One winter, while visiting Berlin, it was -12 outside, and Pier Giorgio gave the coat he was wearing to a poor old man who was shivering on the street. Now *Pier Giorgio* had no coat!

Pier Giorgio called friendship "one of the most beautiful affections." In 1924, Pier Giorgio founded a club called the Tipi Loschi Society, into which he inducted his friends. (*Tipi Loschi* means "The Usual Suspects.") The Society's motto? "Few but good like macaroni." In Italian it rhymes: *"Pochi ma buoni come i maccheroni."*

Pier Giorgio and his friends were silly but serious. Together they went mountain climbing and on alpine picnics. Often Pier Giorgio arranged for Mass in the mountains. When he and his friends were apart, they would write letters, encouraging each other along the path upwards, *verso l'Alto*, as Pier Giorgio would say, *toward Heaven*. They also wrote in a secret code of "booms!" and "salutes," which only they understood. Pier Giorgio's letters included small

gifts: books, rocks from mountain-top treks, dried flowers picked on his hikes, pasta recipes, photographs, promises of prayers while on pilgrimage, bicycle bells. This society of friendship became a communion of pilgrim saints, all helping each other by praying for each other, with Pier Giorgio as their guide.

Little did his friends know, their guide would soon be in Heaven! Pier Giorgio died on July 4, 1925, when he was 24 years old. He had gotten polio while caring for the poor of Turin. With a nearly paralyzed hand and in great pain, he wrote one last letter to his friend Giuseppe Grimaldi. In this letter, he instructed Giuseppe to take the medicine from his coat pocket and give it to Converso. Rather than take the medicine himself, he had saved it for his poor friend. Pier Giorgio died in his mother's arms.

Because he had always worked for the poor in secret, the day of his funeral held many surprises. The poor were surprised to learn their beloved Pier Giorgio was a Frassati, one of the rich and important families in town. And his parents were shocked by the *thousands* of people lining the streets with great emotion as his funeral cortege passed by. These poor people asked the Church to lift Pier Giorgio up as a saintly guide for all of us on our hike to Heaven. He was beatified on May 20, 1990, by Pope John Paul II.

Saint Maximilian Kolbe
(1894–1941)

I T WAS THE LAST DAY OF JULY IN 1941, and it was hot. The Block 14 prisoners of Auschwitz stood at attention in the sun all day. Ten prisoners were being chosen to starve to death as a warning to the others not to try to escape. Among these ten prisoners was Francis Gajownicek. He was sobbing and exclaiming, "My wife! My children!" Suddenly, the prisoner bearing the number 16670 broke rank, pushing through the rows of men toward the commander.

FEAST DAY

August
14

"Stop or be shot!" shouted a guard.

"I want to talk to the commander," the prisoner said, and then politely, "Herr Commandant, I wish to make a request, please."

"What do you want?" said the irritated Commandant Fritsch.

The prisoner made his request: "I want to die in this man's place. I have no wife or children. Besides, I am old and not good for anything. He's in better condition."

Stunned, the commander asked, "Who are you?"

"A Catholic priest."

Everyone standing at attention and watching breathlessly from nearby buildings witnessed this extraordinary exchange.

The Catholic priest was Saint Maximilian Kolbe. In this exchange, we hear Fr. Kolbe offer his life in exchange for that of Francis. Francis was a stranger to Fr. Kolbe, but that was no matter to Fr. Kolbe.

With this act, Fr. Kolbe not only gave Francis his life back, but he showed every person in Auschwitz that they were loved. Remembering Fr. Kolbe's sacrifice, another prisoner later described Fr. Kolbe's sacrifice as an "explosion" of love in the "dark camp night."

Fr. Kolbe and his companions were then shut into cement cells in a building called "the bunker." For the next 14 days, Fr. Kolbe would lead these men in prayer, the Rosary, and song. Their prayer transformed the bunker into a church, with Fr. Kolbe as their priest! They prayed and sang even when their voices were only strong enough to whisper.

Fr. Kolbe died on August 14, 1941, the Eve of the Feast of Mary's Assumption. He called his death "a great work" for God and a mission from Mary Immaculate. Fr. Kolbe received this mission from Mary when he was just a small boy.

As a boy, he was called Raymond, as his parents, Maria and Julius, had named him when he was born. They were a poor but happy family: Maria and Julius, Franciszek, Raymond (Fr. Kolbe), Jozef, Walenty, and Andrzej. Julius was a weaver and Maria worked with textiles, too. It is interesting that they were skilled like Our Lady, because they taught little Raymond to love her. In many pictures of the Annunciation, Mary is spinning wool!

One day, Maria, tired and exasperated, asked her son: "What will become of you?" Ten-year-old Raymond prayed to Our Lady, Mother Mary,

"What will become of me?"

Then she came to me holding two crowns, one white, the other red. She asked me if I was willing to accept either of these crowns. The white one meant that I should persevere in purity, and the red that I should become a martyr.

To Mary, he gave the simple answer, "Yes!"

From that moment on, Raymond was a new boy. It was the beginning of his mission, which he carried out under the name of Maximilian Maria, as a Franciscan priest. Maximilian would tell the whole world about God's love.

He did this in many ways. He started an "army" for Mary, The Militia Immaculata, in which he would fight on behalf of God's love. He started a newspaper called *The Knight of the Immaculata*, in which he could tell people about God's love. Hundreds of thousands of people read this magazine every month! He needed 750 friends to help him print it! After meeting some Japanese people on a train, Fr. Kolbe even traveled very far away from Poland, going to Japan to publish *The Knight* in Japanese for the Japanese people.

When the world went to war, Fr. Kolbe only wanted to fight against the sadness and despair the world then felt. He and his army had two weapons: prayer and love. After he was arrested by the Nazis, Fr. Kolbe continued to wield these weapons every day, helping other men pray, giving them hope, and feeding them his own small rations of food. He fought his greatest battle when he carried out Our Lady's mission and won his red crown, convincing thousands of Auschwitz prisoners of God's love for them. His entire life, Fr. Kolbe had raised the "standard of love on high" for all to see.

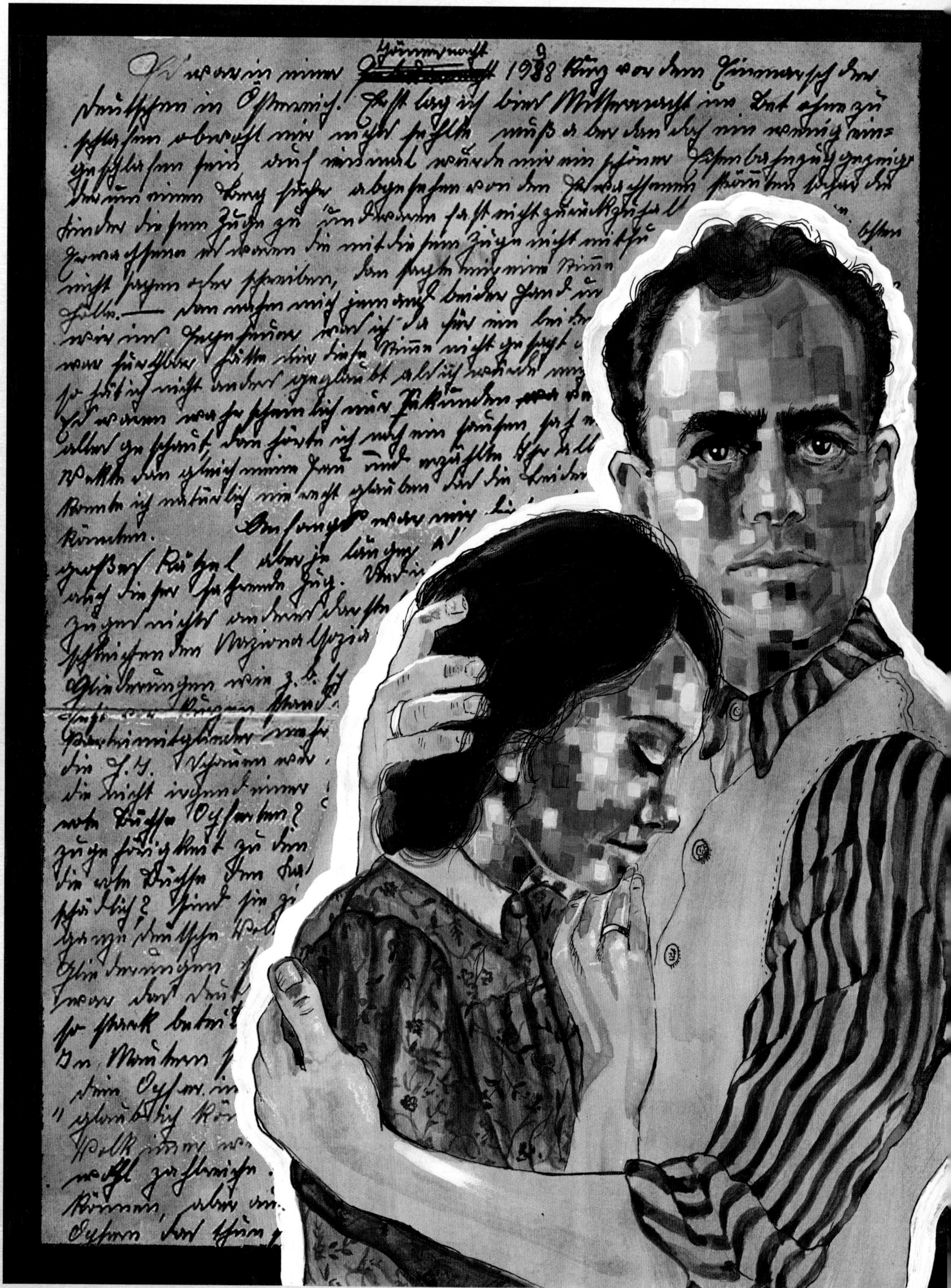

Blessed Franz Jaegerstaetter
(1907–1943)

RANZ AND HIS WIFE, FRANZISKA, lived on a beautiful farm in a little town called Saint Radegund, high in the Austrian Mountains. They had apple trees, and they grew different crops, milked their cows, and took care of their four children. They worked hard, and they were very happy on their farm in the mountains. And they loved each other very much.

FEAST DAY

May
21

But before Franz and Franziska were married, Franz was a little wild. He drove a motorcycle, which was more unusual back then, and he did not think much about his faith.

Franziska's faith, though, was vibrant and beautiful. When they met, Franziska's faith reminded Franz of all that he knew as a little boy about God and His Mother, Mary. Together, they would read the Bible every day, and they would also work hard to thank God by loving their neighbors.

However, in 1938, the neighboring country, Germany, invaded Austria, putting Franz and Franziska's country under the rule of the Nazi Party. The Nazis were not good at loving their neighbors. In fact, they were very unkind to their neighbors. They killed many, many people. Everyone was scared. And everyone was sad.

When the Nazi army called Franz up to fight for them, Franz refused, even though he knew he could be killed for saying "No!" He did not want to fight because that would mean killing his neighbors. He did not want to kill them! He wanted to love them as God said he should.

In 1943 the Nazis arrested Franz for refusing to fight. They put him in prison. And so he had to leave Saint Radegund and his beautiful farm and his beautiful wife and his beautiful children. Franziska had to take care of the farm and their children on her own. It was very hard for both of them! They wrote letters to each other as often as they could.

In many of her letters, Franziska told Franz what their daughters were up to. Sometimes they were being naughty, but usually they were asking for their father to come home.

They missed him. They implored their mother to leave the door unlocked at night, "in case Father will come." Franziska also told Franz what was happening on their farm—if the oats were being sown, or the piglets were being bought, or if the wheat was ready for harvest.

In his letters, Franz would tell Franziska what was happening in the prison, and about the other men he met there. He told her that one of his greatest graces in prison was to still receive the Eucharist. Franz also spent his time writing about his decision not to fight for the Nazis. He asked his readers, "Shouldn't we become even greater saints than the first Christians? Wouldn't it be worthwhile to learn from the lives of the saints?" Even though it was very difficult, Franz looked up to the first Christians, so many of whom were martyrs. He recognized their great ability to love their neighbors, even those who persecuted them, because they loved God. Following in their footsteps, Franz was martyred on August 9, 1943.

Franziska, however, lived to be 100 years old! When she was 97, Franz was beatified. Franziska carried his ashes to the altar of Linz Cathedral, kissing the reliquary urn before handing it to the bishop. How beautiful! And now we can learn about the love of God and the love of neighbor from the lives of Franz and Franziska Jaegerstaetter, saints who have gone before us.

Takashi Nagai, Servant of God (1908–1951)

AKASHI NAGAI was born in a thatched roof hut in Izumo, Japan. Izumo sits beside the Sea of Japan, where the world is beautiful with islands and mountains. Takashi's parents, Noboru and Tsune, both came from samurai families and practiced the Shinto religion. While Takashi would become a medical doctor like his father and while he loved the traditions of his Japanese culture, he would become a Catholic in 1934 at the age of 26.

At the age of 20 Takashi left home to study medicine at Nagasaki University. He also played on the basketball team and joined a poetry writing club. Many of his teachers at the University did not believe God exists. Takashi wrestled with this idea. He read books about prayer by a French scientist named Blaise Pascal. Takashi wrestled with Pascal's words about prayer for several years.

In his second year at the University, Takashi boarded with the Moriyama family. The Moriyama family was one of the ancient Christian families in Nagasaki. The Moriyamas had led the underground Church in Japan for over 250 years!

The story of Christianity in Japan began on the Feast of the Assumption in 1549 when Saint Francis Xavier arrived and proclaimed the gospel for the first time. Other missionaries followed, including St. Maximilian Kolbe who came to Nagasaki almost 400 years later in 1931. The Japanese Christians had endured persecution and martyrdom all those years! Maybe you have heard of Saint Paul Miki and his 25 companions who were crucified on a hill in Nagasaki in 1597.

The Moriyama family, especially their only daughter, Midori, prayed for Takashi. Slowly Takashi learned to pray. He learned to pray the rosary, and to say the very simple prayer, "Jesus, Mary, Joseph." He even came to think of his research and experiments as prayers. Takashi took the name of Paul at his baptism in honor of the martyrs of Nagasaki.

Takashi and Midori were married in August of 1934, two months after his baptism. By then, Takashi had become a radiologist at Nagasaki Hospital, where he was one of the first doctors in Japan to work with X-rays. He used X-rays to detect tuberculosis. He even X-rayed St. Maximilian Kolbe, who suffered from tuberculosis.

At 11:02 a.m. on August 9, 1945, toward the end of the Second World War, the United States dropped an atomic bomb on Nagasaki. It hit near Urakami Cathedral, completely destroying it. Midori Nagai was at home praying her rosary. She died instantly. Takashi was working at the hospital and was badly wounded, but he survived. Their two children were staying in the mountains with their grandmother and escaped harm. Takashi spent the next several days helping the dying and the wounded. As the days passed, Takashi became ill from the radiation. On the brink of death, he prayed to Maximilian Kolbe, and his life was miraculously saved.

On Christmas Eve 1945, Takashi and his friend, Ichitaro Yamada, dug the bell of their beloved Urakami Cathedral from its rubble. By evening, the bell was uncovered and suspended from cedar logs. At 6 p.m., a traditional time of day for the praying of the Angelus, Takashi and Ichitaro rang the bell. To the Christians of Nagasaki, the sound was a miracle. The town wept and prayed the Angelus together!

When Takashi became bedridden because of leukemia, the Saint Vincent de Paul Society built him a 6.5- by 6.5-foot hut, which he named Nyokodo. This means "just as yourself," and was taken from Christ's commandment to love others as yourself. Confined to Nyokodo, Takashi wrote articles and books. With money earned in 1948 by writing these books and articles, he planted 1,000 cherry blossom trees all along the streets of Nagasaki, around the schools and at the new Urakami Cathedral.

Takashi died on May 1, 1951. His funeral Mass ended at noon on May 3rd. Noon is another traditional time for the praying of the Angelus, and so they rang the bells of Urakami Cathedral. All the bells and sirens of Nagasaki sang out in prayerful response to the life of Takashi Nagai.

Saint Gianna Molla
(1922–1962)

O N April 24, 1994, Gianna Molla, a wife, mother, and medical doctor from Milan, Italy, was beatified by Pope John Paul II in Saint Peter's Square. Gianna's husband, Pietro, and three of their children: Pierluigi, Laura, and Gianna Emanuela, were there. Pietro remembers how he felt that day: "I found myself experiencing moments for which I will never be thankful enough to the Lord, the Church, and Gianna. The succession of feelings was incredible, to the point that now and then I had to convince myself that everything was true, that such an extraordinary event was happening to us."

FEAST DAY

April
28

In 2004, Pope John Paul II canonized Gianna. He called her a simple and significant "messenger of divine love" and a "holy mother."

But many years before these happy events, in the Spring of 1970, Bishop Carlo Colombo came to the Mollas' parish to administer Confirmation. After Mass, Bishop Colombo asked Pietro to open the cause for Gianna's beatification. Pietro was very surprised. He "had never heard of a mother becoming a saint!"

But why not? Pietro thought about it.

Pietro still felt Gianna helping him to be happy and helping their children grow in faith and love, even after her death. Pietro compared Gianna's messages of love to radio waves and television signals flowing through the air. We cannot see them, but we know they are there!

Pietro also remembered all the ways Gianna's life had been a message of love. Everyone remembered the great sacrifice she had made for their daughter Gianna Emanuela. Before her daughter was born, Gianna became sick and needed an operation. She refused any treatment that might hurt her unborn daughter, even when it cost her her own life. But Pietro remembered more than this final decision of motherly love. He remembered things like Gianna's "Hymn to the Smile," which she tried to live every day: "To smile at those

109

whom the Lord sends us during the day. . . . We, full of the joy that comes from Jesus, carry joy in our hearts with Jesus. He will be the strength that helps us."

And so, after careful thought, Pietro agreed to open her cause for beatification.

In April of 1994, after Gianna's beatification, her daughter, Gianna Emanuela, wrote: "Since last April I feel like a member of an ever larger family, composed of all who pray to Mamma with me, who confide in her, and feel her beside them as an example to imitate, and I experience the extraordinary sensation of never feeling alone. Within me I feel strength and courage to live; I feel that life smiles at me. . . ." Gianna Emanuela calls her mother "Saint Mom!"

Gianna was from a large family. She was the tenth of thirteen children. Her parents, Maria and Alberto, taught her to love Mass and to love life. Gianna made sure to have lots of fun: dancing, skiing, cooking for friends, going to plays and concerts with Pietro. Life was wonderful! She loved being a doctor. Her smiles were like medicine. And she loved her children. Being a mother made her "perfectly happy." And so she could be happy to give the life she loved so much for her children.

Yes, a mamma can be a saint! And this mamma, Saint Gianna, shows us how the communion of saints is like an extended family, with mothers and fathers and brothers and sisters, all sharing and transmitting the message of divine love.

Dorothy Day, Servant of God
(1897–1980)

EIGHT-YEAR-OLD DOROTHY woke with a fright, her little brass bed sliding all about her dark room. The whole house was shaking! It shook the dishes to pieces and the pictures from the walls.

The great San Francisco earthquake of 1906 left quite an impression on little Dorothy. But not because her house had shaken or the family's dishes were broken. The next morning, her neighborhood was flooded with others whose *homes* had shaken to pieces. Dorothy and her family gave *everything* away to them! This memory of her family's generosity stayed with Dorothy throughout her life.

When Dorothy was 30 years old, she received the greatest gift: her daughter, Tamar Teresa. Becoming a mother made Dorothy supremely happy. "Such a great feeling of happiness and joy filled me," Dorothy writes, "that I longed for Someone to thank, to love, even to worship for so great a good that had been bestowed upon me." She remembered her own family and their generosity. And now she had been given everything! By God, her Father! Dorothy became Catholic shortly after Tamar's birth, in 1927.

Motherhood also led Dorothy to friendship with Saint Thérèse of Lisieux, the Little Flower. Another mother in the hospital introduced Dorothy to this new young saint. Thérèse had died, as Dorothy liked to say, in the same year she herself was born (1897). Dorothy did not know anything yet about this little saint or her little way of love. In fact, she wasn't yet sure she liked this little saint who did little things. Dorothy felt the world had big problems, and lots of them, like war and poverty.

The poor whom Dorothy met had nothing and she wanted to give them everything. She wanted to give them food and clothes and a warm bed. But even more than all these things she wanted to give them God's love and a knowledge of their own dignity. On the feast of the Immaculate Conception in 1932, Dorothy prayed for help in her works of love for the poor. She came home to find a man named Peter Maurin sitting in her kitchen. He

knew he wanted to talk to Dorothy, and to work with her to create a place where it was easy to be good. Peter was an interesting old man with a big heart. He was the youngest of 23 children! And, inspired by Saint Francis of Assisi, he intentionally owned nothing—*nothing*!

Together, Peter and Dorothy imagined a place the poor and homeless could call home. One day Dorothy and Peter put on a pot of coffee and opened the door. Guess what? The poor and the homeless came. And so Dorothy and Peter put on more coffee. They also made bread and soup. And more coffee. And more soup. And more bread. Many people have joined them in their work of loving the poor. By the time Dorothy died in 1980 (Peter had died in 1949), there were 80 such homes with their doors open. These places are called Catholic Worker houses and in them, all across the country, love is given in soup and bread and coffee, clean clothes, and friendship.

Once a rich woman gave Dorothy a big gift—a diamond ring! Dorothy turned around and gave it to the poor woman standing next to her. Just like that! Immediately! No sooner had Dorothy received the diamond than she gave it away. Dorothy said, "Do you suppose God created diamonds only for the rich?"

Saint Thérèse had taught Dorothy and the other Workers that something as small as a cup of coffee or a bowl of soup or a new pair of socks was a really big gift. Love is the measure. As gifts, these small things revealed God's great love. This is something like God giving His love to us in the Eucharist, which Dorothy treasured deeply, and for which she thanked God every day.

Dorothy died in November of 1980. The funeral was meant to be small and quiet: just for family. Her nine grandchildren were to carry her coffin from the Maryhouse Catholic Worker to nearby Nativity Church for the funeral—a walk Dorothy had made many, many times as she went to Mass. Yet on the morning of her funeral, 300 people from the neighborhood came out to accompany her coffin, all streaming along behind it. It was quite a procession! *Everyone* felt Dorothy was their mother, and they had come together to thank God for giving them Dorothy Day, a great and good gift.

Saint Teresa *of* Calcutta
(1910–1997)

NCE THERE WAS A FAMOUS JOURNALIST named Malcolm Muggeridge. In the 1960s Malcolm traveled to India to learn the story of Mother Teresa and her Missionaries of Charity. Malcolm tells us that people would "burst into tears" after visiting Mother Teresa, even if they had only *seen* her during a tea party! They did not have to talk to her! They saw and felt her goodness like the sun's radiance. To be with Mother Teresa was to be with a living saint.

FEAST DAY

September
5

Saints, whether they are canonized or not, are people who live so closely united to the Lord that they radiate God's presence. From a young age this is exactly what Mother Teresa wanted to do with her life.

Mother Teresa was born in Skopje, now in North Macedonia, in 1910 to Nikola and Dranafile Bojaxhiu. Her birth name was Anjezë Gonxhe Bojaxhiu. Anjezë is the name Agnes, and Gonxhe means "rose bud." Her parents taught her to do everything for God alone. Her father told her, "Never eat a single mouthful unless you are sharing it with others."

Anjezë received her First Communion when she was just five and a half. By the time Anjezë was 12 years old she knew she wanted to become a missionary nun. And so when she was 18, she left home. It was hard for her to leave home because she was very happy with her family. Her mother told her, "Put your hand in Jesus's hand, and walk alone with him."

Anjezë joined the Sisters of Loreto. This little "rose bud" wanted to take the religious name of Saint Thérèse of Lisieux, the "Little Flower" who is the Patron of Missionaries, but another sister was already called by this name. Anjezë became Teresa instead.

Teresa took her final vows as a Sister of Loreto in 1937, and spent much of her life with the Sisters teaching at Saint Teresa's school in Eastern Calcutta, India. On Sundays, she went into the homes of the poor. "It was very painful for me," she said, "but at the same time I was very happy when I saw that they are happy because I visited them." One poor mother in particular asked Mother Teresa to keep visiting them: "Oh, Ma, come again! Your smile brought sun into this house!"

In 1946, Teresa heard God speaking to her as she was riding on a train to Darjeeling: "Come be my light" and "carry Me" to the poor. Two years later, Teresa left the beautiful Loreto convent to bring God into the slums of Calcutta. She had just 5 rupees in her pocket (this is like having 7 pennies in the US!). She was poor, but very happy!

By 1950 Mother Teresa had founded the Missionaries of Charity. The Missionaries worked in the slums as God asked, and with those who suffered because there was no one to love them. When Mother Teresa and her Missionaries carried God to the poor, they brought them all the beauty and joy of the universe: love!

Mother Teresa told her Missionaries: "Let Christ radiate and live His life in you." This would not be easy. Mother Teresa once said, "The heat of India is simply burning. When I walk around, it seems to me that fire is under my feet." But a greater fire was in her heart, and Mother Teresa founded schools for children and built a haven for lepers and a Home for the Dying.

Once Malcolm Muggeridge and some men with cameras wanted to film inside the House for the Dying. It was very dark inside because the House only had a few small windows. It seemed impossible to make a movie! But they tried anyway, and guess what? The House for the Dying was filled with the most beautiful light in the movie! The film had miraculously captured the light of God's love radiating in the Home for the Dying.

Mother Teresa believed that we are all called to carry and radiate God's love. We are all meant to be haloed with God's light. She said: "All of us must be saints in this world. Holiness is a duty for you and me. So, let's be saints and so give glory to the Father."

For Further Reading

(Books We Relied Upon While Writing These Stories!)

Pope Saint John Paul II	George Weigel's *Witness to Hope*.
Saint Luke	*Jesus of Nazareth: The Infancy Narratives* by Pope Benedict XVI.
Saint Ignatius of Antioch	Letters of Saint Ignatius of Antioch and *The Golden Legend* by Jacobus de Voragine.
Saint Macrina, the Elder	Gregory of Nyssa's *Life of Saint Macrina, the Younger*.
Saint Anthony of Egypt	Saint Athanasius's *Life of Saint Anthony*.
Saints Monica & Augustine	Augustine's *Confessions*.
Saint Benedict	*The Rule of Saint Benedict* and Gregory the Great's *Life of Saint Benedict*.
Saint Dominic	*The Golden Legend* by Jacobus de Voragine.
Saint Thomas Aquinas	G. K. Chesterton's *Thomas Aquinas*.
Saint Francis of Assisi	*The Little Flowers of Saint Francis*, or *The First Life of Saint Francis* by Thomas of Celano.
Saint Catherine of Siena	Sigrid Undset's *Catherine of Siena*.
Saint Joan of Arc	Mark Twain's *Personal Recollections of Joan of Arc*, or Regine Pernoud's *The Retrial of Joan of Arc*, or Charles Péguy's *The Mystery of the Charity of Joan of Arc*.
Saint Juan Diego	*Nican Mopohua* (English translation by Virgilio Elizondo in *Guadalupe: Mother of the New Creation*).
Saints Zélie & Louis Martin	Dorothy Day's *Thérèse*.
Saint Bernadette	*A Holy Life* or *The Song of Bernadette* by Franz Werfel.
Ven. Augustus Tolton	*From Slave to Priest* by Caroline Hemesath.
Saint Thérèse of Lisieux	Saint Thérèse's autobiography, *The Story of a Soul*.
Bl. Pier Giorgio Frassati	*Letters to His Friends and Family*.

Saint Maximilian Kolbe	*A Man for Others* by Patricia Treece.
Bl. Franz Jaegerstaetter	*The Letters of Franz and Franziska,* translated by Robert Krieg.
Takashi Nagai	*A Song for Nagasaki* by Paul Glynn or *The Bells of Nagasaki* by Takashi Nagai.
Saint Gianna Molla	*Saint Gianna Molla: Wife, Mother, Doctor* by Pietro Molla and Elio Guerriero.
Dorothy Day	*Loaves and Fishes* or *The Long Loneliness,* both by Dorothy Day.
Saint Teresa of Calcutta	*Something Beautiful for God*, by Malcolm Muggeridge, or *Mother Teresa: Come Be My Light,* edited by Brian Kolodiejchuk, M.C.

ABOUT PARACLETE PRESS

PARACLETE PRESS is the publishing arm of the Cape Cod Benedictine community, the Community of Jesus. Presenting a full expression of Christian belief and practice, we reflect the ecumenical charism of the Community and its dedication to sacred music, the fine arts, and the written word.

SCAN
TO
READ
MORE

www.paracletepress.com

Dinner Party with the Saints

WOODEENE KOENIG-BRICKER

author of *365 Saints*